Music

ANCIENTS AND MODERNS

General Editor: Phiroze Vasunia, Professor of Greek,
University College London

How can antiquity illuminate critical issues in the modern world?
How does the ancient world help us address contemporary problems
and issues? In what ways do modern insights and theories shed new
light on the interpretation of ancient texts, monuments, artefacts and
cultures? The central aim of this exciting series is to show how
antiquity is relevant to life today. The series also points towards the
ways in which the modern and ancient worlds are mutually connected
and interrelated. Lively, engaging, and historically informed, *Ancients
and Moderns* examines key ideas and practices in context. It shows
how societies and cultures have been shaped by ideas and debates that
recur. With a strong appeal to students and teachers in a variety of
disciplines, including classics and ancient history, each book is written
for non-specialists in a clear and accessible manner.

Ancients and Moderns Series

The Art of the Body: Antiquity and its Legacy, Michael Squire
Death: Antiquity and Its Legacy, Mario Erasmo
Gender: Antiquity and its Legacy, Brooke Holmes
Luck, Fate and Fortune: Antiquity and Its Legacy, Esther Eidinow
Politics: Antiquity and Its Legacy, Kostas Vlassopoulos
Race: Antiquity and Its Legacy, Denise Eileen McCoskey
Religion: Antiquity and Its Legacy, Jörg Rüpke
Science: Antiquity and its Legacy, Philippa Lang
Sex: Antiquity and Its Legacy, Daniel Orrells
Slavery: Antiquity and Its Legacy, Page Dubois
Sport: Antiquity and Its Legacy, Peter Miller
War: Antiquity and Its Legacy, Alfred S. Bradford

Music

Antiquity and Its Legacy

Eleonora Rocconi

BLOOMSBURY ACADEMIC
LONDON • NEW YORK • OXFORD • NEW DELHI • SYDNEY

BLOOMSBURY ACADEMIC
Bloomsbury Publishing Plc
50 Bedford Square, London, WC1B 3DP, UK
1385 Broadway, New York, NY 10018, USA
29 Earlsfort Terrace, Dublin 2, Ireland

BLOOMSBURY, BLOOMSBURY ACADEMIC and the Diana logo are
trademarks of Bloomsbury Publishing Plc

First published in Great Britain 2024

A catalogue record for this book is available from the British Library.

Library of Congress Cataloging-in-Publication Data
Names: Rocconi, Eleonora, author.
Title: Music : antiquity and its legacy / Eleonora Rocconi.
Description: New York : Bloomsbury Publishing Plc, 2023. | Series: Ancients &
moderns | Includes bibliographical references and index.
Identifiers: LCCN 2023017711 (print) | LCCN 2023017712 (ebook) | ISBN
9781350193819 (hardback) | ISBN 9781350193826 (paperback) | ISBN
9781350193833 (pdf) | ISBN 9781350193840 (ebook)
Subjects: LCSH: Music, Greek and Roman–History and criticism. | Music, Greek
and Roman–Philosophy and aesthetics. | Music–Classical influences.
Classification: LCC ML169 .R635 2023 (print) | LCC ML169 (ebook) | DDC
780.938–dc23/eng/20230502
LC record available at https://lccn.loc.gov/2023017711
LC ebook record available at https://lccn.loc.gov/2023017712

ISBN: HB: 978-1-3501-9381-9
         PB: 978-1-3501-9382-6
         ePDF: 978-1-3501-9383-3
         eBook: 978-1-3501-9384-0

Typeset by RefineCatch Limited, Bungay, Suffolk
Printed and bound in Great Britain

To find out more about our authors and books visit www.bloomsbury.com
and sign up for our newsletters.

In memoriam Andrew Barker (1943–2021)

Series Foreword

Ancients and Moderns comes to fruition at a propitious moment: 'reception studies' is flourishing, and the scholarship that has arisen around it is lively, rigorous, and historically informed; it makes us rethink our own understanding of the relationship between past and present. *Ancients and Moderns* aims to communicate to students and general readers the depth, energy, and excitement of the best work in the field. It seeks to engage, provoke, and stimulate, and to show how, for large parts of the world, Graeco-Roman antiquity continues to be relevant to debates in culture, politics, and society.

The series does not merely accept notions such as 'reception' or 'tradition' without question; rather, it treats these concepts as contested categories and calls into question the illusion of an unmediated approach to the ancient world. We have encouraged our authors to take intellectual risks in the development of their ideas. By challenging the assumption of a direct line of continuity between antiquity and modernity, these books explore how discussions in such areas as gender, politics, race, sex, and slavery occur within particular contexts and histories; they demonstrate that no culture is monolithic, that claims to ownership of the past are never pure, and that East and West are often connected together in ways that continue to surprise and disturb many. Thus, *Ancients and Moderns* is intended to stir up debates about and within reception studies and to complicate some of the standard narratives about the 'legacy' of Greece and Rome.

All the books in *Ancients and Moderns* illustrate that *how* we think about the past bears a necessary relation to *who* we are in the present. At the same time, the series also seeks to persuade scholars of antiquity that their own pursuit is inextricably connected to what many generations have thought, said, and done about the ancient world.

Phiroze Vasunia

Contents

Figures

Acknowledgements

This book has been written in a short time but has had a long gestation. It collects more than twenty years of study and activity aimed at deepening and promoting the topic of ancient Greek music, while also giving me the opportunity to reflect in more depth on the impact of these themes in the history of Western culture. Numerous are the people who have contributed, more or less directly, to its creation and whom I must thank: all my wonderful friends and colleagues of the MOISA Society, whom I do not name individually for reasons of space but who know how much I owe them; my tireless students, both those in the Department of Musicology and Cultural Heritage in Cremona (where I have been working since 1999) and those I have met during my teaching activity in the MOISA Research Seminars, who are the main reason why I wrote this book; the general editor of the series 'Ancients & Moderns', Phiroze Vasunia, who kindly suggested that I contribute to this series, as well as the editorial staff at Bloomsbury, who have been extremely helpful and kind during the whole publication process; last but not least, my friend Maggi Creese, who has added her touch of magic to my English (for whose obscurities, however, I remain solely responsible). A special mention is due to my family, especially my daughter Emma, for having patiently tolerated my absences and anxieties during these last two years: I hope she will enjoy the reading! Finally, my life and career would not have been the same had I not met Andrew Barker, whose loss I suffer more than I can express in words. I dedicate this book to him; unfortunately, he did not have time to read it, but its contents were shared during twenty-five years of uninterrupted collaboration and friendship.

Notes on Dates and Conventions

Dates have been specified as BCE and CE. Proper names of ancient authors, places, historical and mythological characters are mostly given in their Latinate forms, with the exception of those that are best known in their Greek form (e.g. Promomos of Thebes). Texts and fragments of Greek authors have been quoted according to the most recent critical editions and translations, listed in the bibliography.

Introduction: History of an Idea(l)

For a long time, ancient Greek music was an inaudible idea. Until 1581, when the Italian theorist, lutenist and composer Vincenzo Galilei (*c.* 1520–91) published his *Dialogue on Ancient and Modern Music* with the first known examples of 'four ancient chants, composed in the Lydian scale, by one of the ancient Greek musicians' (which only later would be attributed to the composer and kitharode Mesomedes of Crete, *c.* 76–138 CE, cf. *DAGM* 24–5, 27–8), no musical score from antiquity had been discovered, and it would be necessary to wait until the end of the nineteenth century to know a few others. In spite of this, the fascination with this ideal has been extraordinary and its influence on the musical culture of the West undeniable; the greatest part of our musical vocabulary, including the modern words 'music', 'rhythm', 'melody' and many others, derives from Greek via Latin (I.1), while the term *classical* became the label for a musical repertoire that Western culture has canonized as the culmination of its tradition (IV.2). But what is the main contribution of classical antiquity to Western musical culture? What exactly has the reception of ancient Greek music been based on?

The transmission, interpretation, reimagination, rewriting and revival of this ancient idea(l) have gone through various stages throughout history (on revival as theoretical concept see Bithell and Hill 2013). To begin with, I will briefly focus on the cultural implications of some key people and events that may help us contextualize the topics I will address in the following chapters. First of all, we should mention the important role played by the Byzantine humanist and theologian Cardinal Bessarion (1403–72) in collecting and commissioning the manuscripts of a large number of theoretical texts on Greek music, which led to the first circulation of this material in Modern Europe. Among the 750 books that Bessarion donated to the city of Venice in 1468 – the original nucleus of what developed into the Marciana National Library – there are several manuscripts that combine a rich selection of musical theoretical texts from Greek antiquity in a single anthology, running from late classical to Byzantine times (Mathiesen 1988). The codex showing the greatest variety of works is the famous *Marc. Gr. Z.* 322 (= 711), probably commissioned by the cardinal himself in the third quarter of the fifteenth century for his personal library located in Rome (Rocconi 2023). These works soon converged into a kind of canon of ancient treatises on music, including nearly all of what has been preserved in the field, which gradually became available thanks to the activities of large scriptoria where many copies of the same document were produced in a great variety of anthology combinations (Mathiesen 2002). In a cultural climate that looked to the classics as models across multiple domains of cultural production, these theoretical texts aroused great interest not only among scholars but also practical musicians (II.1–2).

A second epochal event in the reception of ancient music was the uncovering of musical instruments and illustrations (paintings and mosaics) within the archaeological excavations at Herculaneum and Pompeii in the late eighteenth century, which exerted a great influence on both organology and visual arts (Castaldo 2020). Before these events, material evidence of ancient musical instruments was totally absent and the themes of inspiration for painters and sculptors were essentially limited to some mythical representations on Roman sarcophagi and statues. After the first discoveries of Herculaneum in 1709/10 and the beginning of systematic archaeological activity – first in Herculaneum (1738) and then in Pompeii (1748) – on the order of Charles of Bourbon (King of Naples from 1734 to 1759), the excavations of the area around Vesuvius had a growing resonance throughout Europe and made Naples a necessary stop on the Grand Tour of Europe. The unearthing of these cities attracted many archaeologists and also scholars of ancient music, such as the English music historian Charles Burney (1726–1814). During his visit to Naples in 1770, he had the opportunity to visit not only the excavations of both sites, but also the Museum Herculanense in the Royal Palace of Portici (established by King Charles to house the findings) and the personal collection of antiquities owned by William Hamilton, the British ambassador to the court of Naples (Melini 2008). Impressed by these first-hand sources, of which he was not allowed to make copies (sketching was prohibited in the museum), he later included plenty of illustrations of musical instruments from Graeco-Roman antiquity in his *General History of Music* (1789) borrowed from other sources (e.g. *Le antichità d'Ercolano esposte*, a volume series published between 1757 and 1792 by the Herculaneum Academy of Archaeology). In this way, he provided images that would be repeatedly copied in later publications and would become archetypes in musical iconography (Blažeković 2012). These discoveries gave also the impulse, in the following century, to the first reproductions of ancient musical instruments, like those constructed by Victor-Charles Mahillon (1841–1924), the founder and first curator of the Musée instrumental du Conservatoire Royal de Musique in Brussels: through imitation of the Pompeian *realia*, he reproduced a horn and some pipes (Vendries 2019, 65–77).

After theory and visual/material evidence, a further important step in the modern reception of ancient Greek music was marked, a century later, by the rediscovery of a number of musical scores, which aroused the scientific interest of scholars and inspired the creativity of contemporary composers and musicians (Solomon 2010). Between the 1880s and the 1890s, important documents came to light, such as the Seikilos inscription (a four-verse song found engraved on a marble column from the Hellenistic city of Tralles, in modern Turkey, *DAGM* 23), the papyrus fragment of Euripides' *Orestes* (an Egyptian papyrus containing part of a choral song from an Euripidean tragedy, *DAGM* 12) and the two Delphic Hymns (two inscriptions containing choral songs addressed to Apollo, *DAGM* 20–1). Media coverage was most intense in the case of the latter: the impact of the discovery in 1893, during the French archaeological excavations at Delphi, of two second-century BCE inscriptions containing two hymns to Apollo notated with music was huge (Solomon 2010, 505–16; Dorf 2019, 21–46). These documents were studied, restored and transcribed by the most important philologists of the time, i.e. Otto Crusius (1857–1918), Henri Weil (1818–1909) and Théodore Reinach (1860–1928, with Bélis 2008). Reinach was particularly active in promoting them; thanks to his support, the first of the two hymns was performed publicly on several occasions between 1894 and 1895. Among these performances, it is worth mentioning the concert at l'École des Beaux-Arts in Paris on 12 April 1894 in the presence of the *Association pour l'encouragement des études grecque* (Reinach 1894), with a newly composed accompaniment by the French composer Gabriel Fauré (1845–1924) who also played the harmonium for the occasion, and an event which occurred shortly afterwards, on 16 June 1894, during the opening ceremony of the first Olympic Congress promoted by the founder of the modern Olympic games Pierre de Coubertin (Miller 2023). On that occasion, the *Hymne à Apollon* was performed in an atmosphere of re-enactment of the ancient Hellenic grandeur.

This renewal of interest in ancient music also fuelled the experimental orientation of the fin-de-siècle theatre that around the same time was starting to encourage outdoor theatrical productions in archaeological venues, with the aim of contextualizing ancient Greek plays within an authentic frame. In 1893, the composer Camille Saint-Saëns (1835–1921) was commissioned to write the music for the revival of the French translation of Sophocles' *Antigone* (prepared many years before by Paul Meurice (1818–1905) and Auguste Vacquerie (1819–95)) which would be staged in 1894 at the Comédie-Française in Paris, with projects to be replicated in the Roman theatre at Orange, in southern France. The cultural atmosphere of the period favoured the Hellenizing approach to Greek tragedy by Saint-Saëns (Huebner 2021), who was asked to replace the incidental music written fifty years earlier by Felix Mendelssohn Bartholdy (1809–47) for the production of the same drama, in German translation, at the Prussian royal court in 1841 (Geary 2006) and later used for the above-mentioned Meurice/Vacquerie translation in its first performance at the Odéon in Paris, in 1844. In the preface of the published score of the play, Saint-Saëns states his debt to the research of the musicologist François-Auguste Gevaert (1828–1908), author of an influential *Histoire et théorie de la musique de l'antiquité* in two volumes (1875 and 1881) which supported an alleged historical continuity between ancient, medieval and modern musical forms. Among the elements derived from antiquity, Saint-Saëns mentions the choice of choral singing in unison, a preference for the Greek modes instead of the modern major/minor patterns, the adoption of an orchestral ensemble meant to replicate ancient sounds (hence the inclusion of flutes, single and double reed instruments, as well as harps as a replacement for the ancient lyre) and the borrowing of an original Greek melody for the final chorus ('Le choeur final est imitè d'un hymne de Pindar', i.e. Pindar's first Pythian ode, nowadays regarded as spurious, cf. II.1). In the union of poetry with music, he says, 'la poèsie tient la première place et la musique ne saurait ètre ici que son auxiliaire' (as advocated by Plato, *Republic* 3.398d, see III.3).

These theatrical experiments confirm the tendency of the nineteenth-century Romantic aesthetics not only to return ancient drama to the theatrical repertoire, but also to revive its musical aspects, considered essential for its appreciation; in 1870, Friedrich Nietzsche (1844–1900) entitled one of the two public lectures given to mark his appointment as Extraordinary Professor of Classical Philology at the University of Basel *The Greek Music Drama* and talked about the drama of antiquity as 'a total work of art' (*Gesamtkunstwerk*, see Nietzsche 2013 [1870])), anticipating those ideas that would find definitive expression in *The Birth of Tragedy from the Spirit of Music* (1872). Nietzsche was here giving implicit support to the ideas of Richard Wagner (1813–83), whose growing fascination with classical Greek drama had inspired in previous decades his important musical theatre reform based on the synthesis of the arts; in the essays *The Artwork of the Future* (1849) and *Opera and Drama* (1851), Wagner had reclaimed the Greek legacy for himself, criticizing earlier attempts to revive Greek tragedy (i.e. Mendelssohn's *Antigone*) and creating his personal reinterpretation of classical antiquity (Lloyd-Jones 1982, 126–42; Geary 2014, 197–226). All these attempts, which aimed at recreating (or, as in Wagner's, rewriting) the drama of ancient Greece as a multimedia performance, converged in the early twentieth century in two parallel artistic projects that, besides contextualizing ancient theatrical performances in their original frame, focused on the re-enactment of their music and dance: 1) the foundation in 1914 of the *Istituto nazionale del dramma antico* ('National Institute of Ancient Drama', better known as INDA) in Siracusa (Italy) under the artistic direction of the classical scholar Ettore Romagnoli (1871–1938), which began its activity with the performance of Aeschylus' tragedy *Agamemnon* (458 BCE) in the ancient Greek Theatre of Siracusa; 2) the revival in 1927 of the Delphic Festival in Delphi (Greece) inspired by the ideas of the poet Angelos Sikelianos (1884–1951) and his wife Eva Palmer (1874–1952), consisting in a series of events which surrounded the performance of Aeschylus' tragedy *Prometheus Bound* (c. 479–424 BCE) in the newly excavated theatre of this important religious centre of antiquity. Although dissimilar in many ways – including their success over time, as the first is still active, while the second was short-lived – both of these projects encouraged directors and musical composers to explore creative solutions for the theatrical staging of ancient plays by engaging with the contemporary artistic and academic investigations on ancient *mousikē*. As far as the first case is concerned, the figure of Romagnoli (philologist and translator with a sensitivity for ancient metrical patterns, which he tried to reproduce in Italian versification, see Troiani 2022a, as well as scholar of ancient music, adviser of composers and composer himself: Troiani 2022b) was essential in proposing an approach to modern performances that, through specific compositional choices and orchestral timbre, could succeed in evoking the archaic atmospheres (see especially Casali 2020, cf. IV.3; other figures of Italian musical modernism grappled with a creative reinvention of antiquity, e.g. Gabriele D'Annunzio, 1863–1938, and Ildebrando Pizzetti, 1880–1968, see Valentini 1992 and Pasticci 2019 respectively). The practice of organizing productions that, relying on a synaesthetic ideal (Piazza 2019), paid great attention to musical and orchestic ingredients continued in the following years; the *INDA* archive collects a lot of musical documents which testify to the number and variety of composers involved in classical performances from 1914 onwards (a conference, titled *Symphonies and Harmonies. From Classical Staging to Today*, devoted to this topic was organized by the institute in 2018). In the case of the two Delphic Festivals that took place in 1927 and 1930, the effort to revive ancient Greek music and dance relied on the belief that it was especially contemporary living practices (Byzantine chant traditions, folk dance and song, merged with the oldest sources) that could allow modern people to recover the authentic *spirit* of Greek culture (Figure 1). The overall project of Eva Palmer Sikelianos and her husband, clearly quite different from a simple archaeological restoration, was to return this spirit of antiquity back to the Greek people, but only after having reshaped it through the lens of modern concerns (on the relationship of this project with other Greek-themed theatrical experiments of the

Figure 1 Dancer (Oceanid) from the chorus of Aeschylus' *Prometheus Bound* at the second Delphic Festival in Delphi (1930). ELIA-MIET Photographic Archive in Athens (Greece). Courtesy of Hellenic Literary and Historical Archive.

early twentieth century, including the choreographed Greek fantasies of the American dancer Isadora Duncan, 1877–1927, see Dorf 2019, esp. 107–38; Dorf 2021).

The brief historical picture I have outlined so far, retracing the fundamental steps in the rediscovery of this cultural heritage throughout the centuries, may have answered – albeit in an approximate and incomplete way – one of my initial questions, that is, on what exactly the reception of ancient Greek music was based. The challenge now is to answer the other question, that is, to try to explain *what* is the main contribution of classical antiquity to the musical culture of Western Europe (leaving aside, due to lack of space and personal skills, the reception of ancient ideas in the music of non-Western cultures). As classical reception is about *our* dialogue with the classical past, the agenda of this book was prompted by some key topics that have emerged in recent scholarly discussions on ancient Greek music. My intention, indeed, is not to talk about the reception of Greek antiquity *in music,* for which I refer the reader to much more authoritative experts than myself (e.g. Levidou, Romanou and Vlastos 2016). I rather wish to focus, more broadly, on the legacy of ancient Greek music and musical ideas *in musical culture.* My main goal is to identify their persisting contribution to modern cultural debates within the realms of Classics, Musicology, Philosophy, Aesthetics, Anthropology, Performance and Cultural Studies.

To do this, I first introduce some of the longest-lasting musical concepts that were developed in the Greek world, re-examining and reassessing their meaning and transformation throughout antiquity and showing their relevance to some ongoing discussions about the role of music in society (Chapter 1). Chapter 2 deals with music theory, which forms the greatest part of the surviving documentary evidence on ancient music; after summarizing the evidence for its origin and development within the broadest context of ancient philosophical and scientific thought, I devote special attention to those ideas that provided the foundations for speculations and experiments of various kinds in later centuries. Chapter 3 focuses on some of the issues originally addressed in ancient times that have most influenced subsequent discussions in the field of musical aesthetics and, more recently, neuroaesthetics. Chapter 4 seeks to identify some recurring (often oppositional) patterns that, since classical antiquity, have characterized the cultural history of music. To conclude, I formulate some hypotheses concerning the possible reasons behind the lasting attraction of Greek *mousikē* over time, which has been an inexhaustible source of inspiration for musicians, theorists, scholars and antiquarians over the centuries, also trying to stimulate the debate on the role that ancient ideas and practices – decontextualized from their historical setting – can have in the contemporary world. These reflections certainly do not claim to be exhaustive; my hope is to give food for thought for further discussions.

1

Key Terms and Concepts

1. The cultural notion of *mousikē*

Ancient Greeks were in the habit of tracing the origin of their objects, techniques and cultural practices to divine or heroic *prōtoi heurētai* (i.e. 'first discoverers'), and music was no exception.[1] Musical instruments and genres were traditionally regarded as originating from deities or heroes who, after discovering their archetypes in the natural world, elaborated and delivered their mimetic reproduction to human beings, thus marking the transition to a sphere of culture and civilization. The most illustrious examples of divine musical craftsmanship include the construction of the tortoiseshell lyre by the god Hermes, beautifully narrated in all its technical details in the *Homeric Hymn to Hermes* 24–61 (late sixth century BCE? Cf. Vergados 2013; Romani Mistretta 2017), or the transformation of the Gorgons' lament into the instrumental melody called 'many-headed air' (*polykephalos nomos*) by the goddess Athena, described by Pindar (*c.* 518–438 BCE) in the act of interweaving (*diaplekein*) the monstrous dirge into a product of her divine handicraft (*Pythian* 12.19–24, with Gentili and Luisi 1995; Steiner 2013). This link between music and the divine was also ubiquitous in cults and the religious practices of Greek antiquity (Power 2022).

The transition from a world of natural sounds to an array of cultural practices became plainly evident in the very name *music*.[2] This word made explicit the connection with the Muses (Figure 2), goddesses often invoked by ancient poets as the source of their inspiration (their invocation persisting as a literary convention up to recent times, after their cult had long since expired), sometimes even standing, metonymically, for song itself.[3] The coinage *mousikē* originated, no earlier than the late sixth century BCE, as an adjective whose suffix -*ikē* implies the word *technē* (see below) like other terms introduced shortly after it, e.g. *grammatikē* and *rhetorikē* (IV.4). It is used to indicate the 'art of the Muses', that is, all the (collective) artistic activities in the Muses' domain – song, dance, poetry, instrumental accompaniment and solos – as well as an intricate set of values, from refinement to education, connected to their prototypical skills and powers (see, e.g., Murray 2014, 2015 and 2020, with further bibliography).[4]

In ancient Greece these goddesses, daughters of Zeus and Mnemosyne (whose name means 'Memory', deemed essential in an oral culture, see Curtis and Weiss 2021), were conceived as a plurality operating as a unity; their names and number were originally fluid and

Figure 2 Muses attending the procession for the marriage of the hero Peleus to the nymph Thetis. Attic black-figure volute krater (François Vase), painted by Kleitias (*c.* 570 BCE): Florence (Italy), Museo Archeologico Nazionale (MAF) inv. 4209.

closer associations with particular arts or fields of knowledge established only in later periods.[5] This probably explains why the term *mousikē* (singular) could convey such a broad and dense notion, laying the foundation for the unitary concept of music later developed by Western European cultures.[6] Indeed the cultural notion of *mousikē* is a peculiarly Greek social construct which originated in a specific context, i.e. the so-called *song culture* of the archaic and classical times (for the expression *song culture*, see Herington 1985): this is the context in which the need for labelling musical performances as an organized set of cultural activities, occurring on specific religious and social occasions, was gradually felt.[7] Nevertheless this notion, while redefining itself over time, survived social and cultural changes by endowing Western languages with a comprehensive term, capable of encompassing various musical genres and styles and of expressing the numerous, sometimes conflicting values linked to this multifaceted phenomenon.

The socially constructed meaning of *mousikē* relies on assumptions that already appear clearly in the proem to Hesiod's *Theogony* (seventh century BCE), a poem describing the origins and genealogies of all the Greek deities, whose opening lines are the foundational text for the Muses' mythology. It is here that, for the first time in our sources, Muses are given individual names:

Come then, let us begin [sc. our song] from the Muses, whose hymns delight the great heart of Zeus their father in Olympus, speaking of what is, what will be, and what has been, agreeing with their voices. Their sweet sound flows tireless from their mouths, and the home of their father, Zeus the loud thunderer, rejoices at the goddesses' lily-like voice as it is scattered. The peaks of snowy Olympus and the homes of the gods resound. Uttering their immortal voice they praise first in song the revered race of gods from the beginning [. . .].

There are their gleaming dance-places and their beautiful homes. With them the Graces and Desire live in joyous festivities. And uttering through their mouths a lovely voice, they sing in praise of the customs of all and the noble practices of the immortals, uttering a most lovely sound. Then they went to Olympus, rejoicing in their beautiful voice, with undying song and dance: the dark earth rang about them as they sang their hymn, and a lovely clamour rose from beneath their feet as they went to their father. He it is that reigns in heaven, holding the lightning and the glittering thunderbolt, having conquered his father Cronos by his strength. And he distributed everything fairly to each of the immortals and announced their prerogatives.

Of these things, then, the Muses sang, the Muses who live on Olympus, the nine daughters begotten by great Zeus – Clio, Euterpe, Thalia, Melpomene, Terpsichore, Erato, Polhymnia, Ourania and Calliope: she is the most eminent of them all, for she ministers to revered kings.[8] [...] He whom the Muses love is happy, for a sweet voice flows from his mouth. For if someone has grief in his new-troubled spirit, and is in fear, distressed in his heart, still, when a singer, a servant of the Muses, hymns the glories of men of the past and of blessed gods who live on Olympus, at once he forgets his miseries and resembles his troubles no more: the gifts of the goddesses swiftly turn him another way.

Hesiod, *Theogony* 36–103, transl. Barker 1984

As pointed out by several scholars, the speaking names occurring at vv. 77–9 are built upon the talents and actions attributed to the Muses in the previous verses (on this passage, see especially Harriott 1969, 16; Vergados 2014; Semenzato 2017, 100–3; Murray 2020, 16). More precisely:

- the main activities of these goddesses are song (*molpē*) and dance (*choreia, choros*);

Melpomenē = 'Singing'	*Terpsichorē* = 'Delighting in Dance'
66: 'they sing' (*melpontai*)	7: 'they dance' (*chorous enepoiēsanto*)
69: 'with undying song and dance' (*molpēi*)	63: 'their gleaming dance-places' (*choroi*)[9]

- their performances occur during public festivities (*thaliai*) in honour of the celestial (*ouranioi*) gods;

Thaleia = 'Festive'	*Ouraniē* = 'Heavenly'
65: 'in joyous festivities' (*en thaliēis*)	71: 'He it is that reigns in heaven' (*ouranōi*)

- their activities are meant to celebrate (*kleiein, hymnein*) as well as to delight (*terpein*) the deities;

Kleiō = 'Celebrating'	*Polhymnia* = 'Many Hymning'	*Euterpē* = 'Well Delighting' (cf. *Terpsichorē*)
44: 'they praise (*kleiousin*) first in song the revered race of gods'	11: 'hymning (*hymneusai*) Zeus [...] and Hera [...] and Athena [...]' etc. 37: '[...] whose hymns delight the great heart of Zeus'	37: 'they delight (*terpousi*) the great heart of Zeus'
66f.: 'they sing in praise (*kleiousin*) of the customs of all and the noble practices of the immortals'	50f.: 'they hymn (*hymneusai*) the race of men and strong Giants'	51: 'they delight (*terpousi*) the heart of Zeus'
100: 'when a singer [...] hymns the glories (*kleia*) of men of the past and of blessed gods'	70: 'they sang their hymn' (*hymneusais*)	

- the voice of the Muses, or the thud produced by their feet when dancing, is beautiful (*kalos*) and lovely (*eratos*).

Kalliopē = 'Beautiful Voiced'	*Eratō* = 'Lovely'
68: 'rejoicing in their beautiful voice' (*opi kalēi*)	65: 'uttering [...] a lovely voice' (*eratēn* [...] *ossan*)
	67: 'uttering a most lovely sound' (*epēraton ossan*)
	70: 'a lovely clamour (*eratos* [...] *doupos*) rose from beneath their feet'

Taken as a whole, the Muses thus appear as the embodiment of the most relevant aspects of poetic and musical activity, which they do not only patronize but also perform in first person. They are bestowers of pleasure and happiness, they have an immortalizing and celebrating power and they possess the capacity to preserve order and harmony, all elements that will be repeatedly and variously mentioned by later authors when defining the role of musical art(s) and its practitioners. Moreover, thanks to the supernatural authority of these goddesses, their actions turn into a paradigmatic model for the human poet who, through his connection with the divine, becomes able himself to celebrate the glories of deities and heroes and to relieve pain and suffering.[10]

Besides being perceived as a gift of the gods, however, *mousikē* was also a *technē*, having its foundations in materiality and craftsmanship.[11] The Greek term *technē* is hard to translate by any single term, in English or any other modern language; it is comparable neither to pure 'craftsmanship' nor to the modern idea of 'art' (the latter heavily influenced by the Romantic ideology which tends to associate it with objects of properly aesthetic value: see Parry 2014; Kjeller Johansen 2021).[12] The ancient artists (*technitai*, in Greek) are rather regular practitioners of a specialist skill, a *know how* that can be applied to several fields, from weaving to rhetoric (e.g. Plato, *Gorgias* 449c–d), including both a productive expertise and a theoretical understanding of the subject involved (hence not in sharp opposition with *epistēmē*, cf. II.1).[13] The professional status of musicians, including poets, singers and instrumentalists, is well attested since the archaic age, when we are informed about the existence of patrons – be they tyrants, aristocrats or public institutions (Gentili 1988, ch. 8) – and the increase in opportunities for musical competition, due to the establishment of many religious festivals throughout the Greek world (Chaniotis 2011; Martin 2015). However, it was only when *mousikē* become a common term in the current language that the specific field of this expertise starts to be more sharply defined and openly claimed by its artists, paving the way for a more marked professionalism of the latter.

The debate about the notion of *technē* – which intensified between the fifth and fourth century BCE, especially in philosophical contexts, see I.3 – undermined the educational role of activities related to the Muses. Soon enough, a more abstracted meaning of *mousikē* began to be discussed; in philosophical contexts, *mousikē* was praised as a special form of knowledge, a prerequisite for philosophy (cf. Plato's designation of philosophy as the highest form of *mousikē* in *Phaedo* 4.61a). As music theory developed, the theoretical side of this *technē* was gradually explored by musicians themselves. Famous is Plato's ridicule of their attempts to measure sounds and intervals by torturing musical instruments in public demonstrations before an audience in *Republic* Book 7:[14]

> Their behaviour is quite ridiculous, when they name some things *pyknōmata* (i.e. sounds which are 'closely spaced or packed' in terms of pitch) and incline their ears as if hunting out a sound from next door, some of them asserting that they can still just hear a sound in between, and that that is the smallest interval, by which measurement is to be made [...] those worthy persons who bully the strings and interrogate them with torture, racking them on the *kollopes* (i.e. tuning pegs).
>
> Plato, *Republic* 7.531a–b, transl. Barker 1989

This growing transformation of *mousikē* into an intellectual activity[15] – i.e. into an *epistēmē*, see I.3 – would later culminate in its inclusion among the theoretical disciplines of the so-called *quadrivium*, whose first sketch may be dated back to Plato's *Republic* (7.530c–531c). Here music theory, more precisely harmonic science, is listed among the fundamental disciplines for educating the philosopher kings in order to ascend to wisdom (Barker 2007, 315–18).

2. Ancient *musicking*

In recent decades, musicology has made great efforts to go beyond the idea of performance as mere reproduction of written texts (i.e. scores). When arguing against such a restricted view, resulting from the almost exclusive focus of the discipline on Western classical music until recent years,[16] scholars have discussed the (late) emergence of the concept of *musical work* and its consequences for the modern experience of music (Goehr 1992), affirming the need to shift from a text-based to a performance-based understanding of musical phenomena (Cook 2013). Some of the critical reflections which have matured within these studies are particularly interesting for re-evaluating the legacy of the ancient notion of *mousikē*. They allow us both to better understand how profoundly the meaning of this term has changed in the cultural history of the West and to clarify some key aspects of its historical contextualization in classical antiquity.

The reification of the notion of music, harshly criticized for imposing a significant restriction on the semantic potential of the term, is at the core of Christopher Small's book titled *Musicking: The Meanings of Performing and Listening* (1998), which is one of the most intriguing contributions to the musicological debate on the topic. In this work the author points out that music is not a *thing* at all, but an *activity*: 'performance', he says, 'does not exist in order to present musical works, but rather, musical works exist in order to give performers something to perform', as 'the fundamental nature and meaning of music lie not in objects, not in musical works at all, but in action, in what people do' (Small 1998, 8). Hence the proposal to introduce the new term *musicking* into musicological vocabulary, from the verb 'to music', shifting the focus from music conceived as an *object* (i.e. a noun) towards music conceived as a *process* (i.e. a verb; cf. LeVen 2020, 2–8).[17] This – misleading, in Small's opinion – process of abstraction, which is accused of being the major obstacle to our understanding of musical phenomena, probably had its origin in Greek antiquity (Small blames Plato for this!). A role in this process was certainly played by the introduction and spread of the term *mousikē*, an adjective gradually transformed into a noun, thus coming to indicate a *thing*. But a series of factors, such as the relatively late invention of musical writing systems (not earlier than the fifth century BCE, see Hagel 2020),[18] the improvisational character of some genres (with the consequent lack of the *work concept* that is typical of Western art music)[19] and the pervasiveness of musical events in many contexts of ancient religious and social life, suggest that, at least throughout the classical age, *mousikē* was never intended as a pure abstraction, not even by those philosophers who were most interested in it as a speculative phenomenon.

The idea of music as a performing art, i.e. as an act of *musicking* thought not only to possess but also *create* relevant meanings for the community involved, informs the contents of Plato's last dialogue, titled *The Laws* (mid-fourth century BCE). In this work, where Plato describes the recommended political structure of an imaginary colony (named Magnesia) to be founded in Crete, *mousikē* is always presented as an activity with an important social and educational role. The main focus is on *choreia*, a term whose meaning includes 'choral dancing and singing' (*orchēsis te kai ōidē*, 2.654b3),[20] described as a participatory event with specific ethical goals. Plato believes that, thanks to their active involvement as performers, the citizens of Magnesia can become accustomed to what is fine (*to kalon*, cf. III.4) in music – and, consequently, in human life (654c–d) – from a very young age and are therefore more easily led to virtues, which take root in their souls as they continue and maintain musical education throughout their existence (666a–e).[21]

Indeed, in archaic and classical times choral performances took place on public occasions of various kinds. There were several kinds of song, which differed both according to the purpose and context in which they were performed (e.g. victory songs, wedding songs and others) and to the age and gender of the performers (boys, girls, adult men and women). Specific genres were performed for each god: dithyrambs in honour of Dionysus, paeans addressed to Apollo and so on (for a panoramic survey of Greek *choreia*, see Weiss 2020, with further bibliography).[22] The beautiful image that Plato uses here to describe the origin of *choreia* not only confirms the well-attested connection of musical practices with deities, but also emphasizes some characteristics inherent in choral activity that, besides recalling the Hesiodic description of the Muses, add further interesting elements. Choruses, he says, derive their name from the 'joy' (*chara*) that is natural to them (2.654a, cf. Hesiod, *Theogony* 36ff.: 'the home of their father [...] *rejoices* at the goddesses' lily-like voice').[23] They are a gift from the gods who, 'in pity for the race of men, born to toil, established for them as respites from their labours the festivals of thanksgiving to the gods', granting them as companions in their feasts the Muses with their leader Apollo, and Dionysus, 'so that they might be set right again, along with the nourishment that comes from joining in festivals with the gods' (2.653d).[24] In this description, not only the human beings, but also the divine figures are described as *enacting agents* of musical events, suggesting that the modern textualist paradigm on which musicology has been traditionally based cannot be applied to ancient *mousikē*, whose meanings and values were rather actively constructed by an ongoing interaction between the performers and their audience (Goldhill and Osborne 1999).

Despite the great importance of performative aspects in ancient Greek poetry, however, the survival of the texts alone has encouraged a strictly literary approach to them which still persists today. This has led many scholars (especially classical philologists) to ignore the intrinsic musicality of ancient poetic texts[25] and to dismiss the role of performance in the poetic experience of the past (on continuity and change in the experience of poetry throughout the centuries, from Greek antiquity to the English Renaissance, see Attridge 2019). This attitude began at least as early as Aristotle who, in the *Poetics*, introduced a bookish approach to what we now call Greek *literature*.[26] In his analysis of ancient tragedy, for instance, he shows an almost exclusive interest in the technical rules governing dramatic structure, dismissing aspects related to its staging.[27] Or, when reporting that tragedy is considered vulgar in comparison with epic, he rejects this argument on the grounds that we should not criticize the art of drama *per se*, but only its delivery (*Poetics* 26.1462a2–9). But in tragic performances, as in any other kind of musical poetry, both mimetic and diegetic, the narrative progressions were made more effective by the action of music (as incidentally suggested by Aristotle too),[28] i.e. by its *musicking*, which marked the rhythm of represented or narrated events over time[29] and enhanced the emotional reaction of the audience (as happens to us too when we watch a movie with a good soundtrack).[30] The Greek experience of poetry, whatever its genre – melic poetry, tragedy, comedy and so on – was clearly based on music as a *process*.[31] It follows that, if we rely on the authority of the texts alone, unfortunately we lose the deeper meaning of ancient *mousikē*.

3. The educational value of music: From *mousikē paideia* to *quadrivium*

The debate about the value of music in education runs through history and is ongoing.[32] Current discussions mainly focus on questions related to modern globalization, such as cultural diversity, multicultural and intercultural matters, or world music pedagogy (see, e.g., Schippers 2010), with the more general purpose of addressing issues of identity and inclusion and, hence, making musical education more open and responsive to broader social concern. The social value of music, both practical and theoretical, has been a subject of investigation since Greek antiquity; due to its importance in the culture of the time, it was natural for *mousikē* to draw the attention of intellectuals and philosophers. Some of the reflections that emerged in their discussions were particularly compelling and continued to influence the debate on these issues in the following centuries.

Paideia ('education') was a crucial ingredient in ancient philosophers' idea of a well-governed *polis*, conceived as a community of free people (Aristotle, *Politics* 3.1279a22, cf. 7.1332a32ff.). This is the reason Plato incorporated educational concerns into his broader

Figure 3 Man offering a lyre and a ball (symbols of education) to a boy. Attic red-figure column krater (*c.* 475–465 BCE): New York (USA), Metropolitan Museum 41.162.86.

philosophical and political agenda, the aim of which was the achievement of a state based on justice and virtue. In the educational framework outlined in his dialogues, *mousikē* plays a leading role since it is one of the most effective means through which the Hellenes could convey and reinforce their values.[33] But it was not only participation in choruses that was essential to build the identity of the community in terms of culture, ethnicity and gender (see I.2 and IV.3); the role of *mousikē* was certainly greater (Raffa 2020).[34] Learning music began from a younger age with the instruction of the *kitharistēs*, a 'lyre teacher' who trained children, from the age of about seven, in the practice of the lyre and singing (Figure 3). Thanks to this early training, adult citizens could actively participate in civic and religious rituals, e.g. the symposium (lit. 'drinking party'), the most significant context for the performance and transmission of ancient Greek poetry.[35] The contribution of *mousikē* in defining human beings as active members of society stimulated the first pioneering efforts to find theoretical justifications for its inclusion in educational programmes. At the basis of Plato's and others' reasoning lies the principle that music may influence the character of those who are exposed to it by virtue of its 'psychagogic' power (lit. 'leading' or 'persuading the soul', from *psychē* = 'soul' + *agein* = 'to lead, to carry', cf. I.4 and III.2). Modern philosophers of education would certainly question the controversial principle that shaping the soul (i.e. the mind) of their pupil should be the main goal of any institutional education (which, in this way, would reflect the interests of a powerful cultural elite); the pedagogical trends of today rather prefer a type of education that allows students to strengthen their critical powers and to develop independent research skills (Scheffler 1989 [1973]).[36] An important change in this educational model took place in the second half of the fifth century BCE; the establishment of new didactic programmes by the sophists (intellectuals who taught privately in aristocratic houses for a fee and disseminated their knowledge of any kind of *technē* through speeches in public spaces, where they honed their rhetorical skills, cf. IV.4) was seen as a challenge to traditional values and slowly undermined the primacy of *mousikē paideia* (Pelosi 2017; Novokhatko 2020). An echo of the growing debate on the usefulness of musical instruction is attested in Aristotle's *Politics* Book 8, where he repeatedly asks if *mousikē* – even in its most practical aspects – should be included in the educational curriculum of the *eleutheroi* (i.e. the 'free citizens') and, if so, why.[37]

The first points he makes, in agreement with Plato, are the following: 1) education should be provided by the state and not be private (a topic still debated in current discussions about equal opportunity and access to education, though on completely different cultural premises), as 'matters of public interest ought to be under public supervision' (1337a27);[38] 2) education can be obtained through learning and habituation (a form of non-associative learning also widely investigated by modern psychology: Destiyanti and Setiana 2020), since 'men learn some things by practice, others by precept' (1332b10f., cf. Plato, *Laws* 2.653a–c). Aristotle differentiates school disciplines by presenting a programme in which reading and writing, included under the term *grammatikē*, are perfectly distinct from *mousikē* (hence testifying to the increasing literacy of fourth-century BCE culture), not only as regards their contents but also the role they should have in education (1337b23ff.).[39] While *grammatikē* falls into the category of the useful (*chrēsimoi*) disciplines, the purpose of music, he says, needs clarification: its main goal is 'to beautifully occupy leisure' (*scholazein kalōs*), i.e. free time, which is the purpose of a good, i.e. virtuous life (1337b27ff., cf. 1334a2ff.).[40] Aristotle here is not referring to music as amusement or relaxation (which may also be one of its purposes, as we are told in 1339a16), but to its contribution to the way of life (*diagōgē*) of men who, thanks to the musical training received in their early years, become willing to live and act in morally significant ways.[41] There are many philosophical implications in the complex reasoning developed here (see, e.g., Destrée 2017; Rocconi 2019a; Roochnik 2022). For our purposes, the most important is the fact that the ethical value Aristotle attributes to musical training (which can lead young people to acquire virtuous habits) is based on the effectiveness of the highly mimetic power of scales and rhythms, the strictly technical components of *mousikē*, which can represent good or bad characters much better than any other object of perception (III.3).[42] By highlighting the benefits of the *practical* experience of music, Aristotle provides evidence for the growing separation of the practical and theoretical aspects of *mousikē*, a process that had already been set in motion by Plato (I.1). In fact he clearly acknowledges the benefits of singing and playing instruments (1340b31–3: 'Considerations of this sort show that music should be taught in such a way that the pupils take part in its practice'), even if he warns the pupils against an over-development of professional abilities, which are not appropriate for free men:

> We reject, then, a technical education in instruments and in performance on them. By 'technical' education we mean that which equips people for competitive performances. *The player does not pursue it to improve his own virtue, but to promote the pleasure of the listeners* – a depraved pleasure, at that – and for this reason we reckon the task to be appropriate not to free men, but menials.
>
> Aristotle, *Politics* 8.1341b8–14, transl. Barker 1984, italics mine

By saying that the aim of 'participation in practice' (*metechein tōn ergōn*) should be the development of judgment, 'the capacity to judge what is good (*kala krinei*) and to enjoy things correctly (*chairein orthōs*), as a result from what they learned when they were young' (1340b35–9), Aristotle still values musical practice, as in the past, recognizing its contribution to virtue. But such a traditionalist approach to musical education had been evidently plunged into serious crisis, if he felt the need to defend it. The tendency to develop a purely speculative approach to musical learning, which would eventually lead to the inclusion of music – as a theoretical discipline – in the *quadrivium* (the medieval curriculum that comprised arithmetic, geometry, astronomy and harmonic science as preparation for the study of philosophy and theology), was already underway (II.1).[43]

The rediscovery of Aristotle's ideas on the value of music in education then occurred at the beginning of the Renaissance (Restani 2011b), when fresh attention to political and ethical themes revitalized the interest in some Aristotelian works such as the *Politics* and *Nicomachean Ethics*, now interpreted as a useful guide to practical life.[44] In a cultural context in which the humanists (i.e. 'those devoted to the *studia humanitatis*', so called in the belief that they made men more human, that is, virtuous and wise)[45] had taken over the role of educators of princes and nobles, Book 8 of the *Politics* offered a pedagogical model that included *practical* music, rather than *musica speculativa*, i.e. music as one of the quadrivial mathematical sciences (Gallo 1995, 62f.; Gallo 1998; Hankins 2015, 233ff.).[46] The Aristotelian concerns related to *paideia* provided material for discussion in several educational treatises (called 'mirrors for princes', *specula principum*) written between the thirteenth and fifteenth centuries, in which the 'free men' of Aristotle's *Politics* were replaced by the nobles and civic leaders of the period. One of the earliest and most influential among these treatises was the work titled *On the Rule of Princes* (*De regimine principum*) by Giles of Rome (*c.* 1243/47–1316),[47] the scholastic theologian who mediated the Aristotelian thought concerning moral philosophy and politics to the Latin West (Coleman 1998; Briggs and Eardley 2016). His treatise is a work of political advice for rulers, written for (and dedicated to) the future King of France, the young Philip the Fair. Giles' concerns about the role of music in the education of the future king are clearly based on the Aristotelian model. The treatise explicitly prescribes the teaching and exercise of music (*practica musica*) which must accompany all the prince's life since, as Aristotle said in the *Politics*, 'it serves good habits' (*deservit ad bonos mores*, cf. *De regimine* 310): up to the age of seven, besides fables and stories the prince should listen to 'some respectable songs' (330: *alicui cantus honesti*); from seven to fourteen, he must be trained in singing (333: *quadam modulantia vocum*); after the age of fourteen, when he has fully developed the ability to reason, he can finally cultivate polyphonic music (337: *in consonantia vocum*).[48]

During the Renaissance, however, Aristotle's authority went beyond the definition of the educational programme of the upper classes; his ideas were also reflected in the first attempts to institutionalize musical teaching in Europe.[49] For instance, Bruni's influential translation of the *Politics,* completed between 1436 and 1438, seems to have inspired the systematic instructional work of Pope Eugene IV, dedicatee of the translation, who, between 1435 and 1446, decided to establish the so-called *scuole eugeniane* in many Italian cities.[50] These cathedral schools of chant and grammar were free and open also to boys of modest origin – therefore having an important social function at the time – and soon became the embryonic nucleus of the future musical chapels, also contributing to the development of professionalism in music, in Italy and beyond (Cattin 1981, 21f.; Da Col 2018, 240).[51] If, in the fourth century BCE, Aristotelian ideas on musical education, which were not socially inclusive, had clearly been projected towards the past, centuries later they gave great impulse to the establishment of modern musical teaching in Europe.

4. Music therapy and healing harmony

In the preface of his successful book *Musicophilia* (2007), the neurologist Oliver Sacks observes that, if in the past neuroscience has rarely been concerned with music (at least not before 1977, when Macdonald Critchley and Ronald Henson published their influential book *Music and the Brain*, which paved the way for a growing interest of modern scholarship on the topic), the situation has changed radically in recent decades. Thanks to new technologies, it has finally become possible to observe the brain of a human being while listening to and imagining music, thus allowing for a better understanding of its great appeal and powerful effects on us (Thaut and Hodges 2021). The situation has further improved since then. Music therapy programmes are now universally accepted as treatments for disorders of various kinds and have become part of specific curricula in university courses worldwide.[52]

The ancient Greeks explored this subject extensively. *Mousikē* was not only thought to impose a kind of consoling order onto all aspects of existence, including suffering and death; it was also strongly advocated as a means for restoring the balance in the human soul and for curing specific diseases in the body, such as sciatica and epilepsy.[53] We find evidence for the therapeutic use of music since the Homeric poems, where an enchantment (*epaoidē*, lit. 'song sung to or over' someone or something) stops the blood that flows from Odysseus' wound (*Odyssey* 19.455–8), and many are the references throughout ancient literature to the contribution of music in treating disorders of various kinds (Provenza 2020).

One of the most frequently recurring concepts in the sources that discuss music therapy is the notion of catharsis, whose foundations in Greece are both medical and religious. The Greek term *katharsis* originally described the liberation of the body from pathological excesses (*kathairein* means 'to cleanse', 'to purge'). The religious use of music with this specific purpose was already present in the *Iliad* (1.472–4), where a sung supplication in the form of a paean (a religious song usually addressed to Apollo and distinguished by the refrain *iē paian*)[54] praises the god, in his role as healer, to persuade him to stop the plague.[55] Evidence for the traditional use of music for cathartic purposes connects it to the earlier Pythagoreans, although specific information in this regard is provided by much later sources, such as the Neoplatonic works *The Life of Pythagoras* by Porphyry of Tyre (*c.* 233–305 CE) and *On the Pythagorean Way of Life* by Iamblichus of Chalcis (*c.* 245–325 CE). In the latter we are told that Pythagoreans sang paeans 'to induce feelings of joy, and to become graceful and rhythmical' (*On the Pythagorean Way of Life* 110, transl. Dillon and Hershbell 1991). Great was the trust they placed in medical treatment (*iatreia*) through music, deemed capable of inspiring order (*taxis*) and of healing body and soul, especially emotions (*pathē*): 'there are certain melodies created for the soul's emotions which, in fact, were designed to be most helpful against despondency and mental suffering; and again, other melodies against rages, angers, and against every mental disturbance of the soul so afflicted' (*On the Pythagorean Way of Life* 111).[56] The first testimony in which music therapy is explicitly associated with these communities (mainly operating in Magna Graecia, the cradle of Pythagoreanism) is a fragment of Aristoxenus of Tarentum (*c.* 370/65–? BCE) attesting that the Pythagoreans 'used medicine for the purification (*katharsis*) of the body, and music for that of the soul' (fr. 26 Wehrli). As recent scholars have convincingly argued, it is unlikely that these early communities had ever elaborated a fully developed theory of catharsis as the articulated theories later attested in Plato and Aristotle (although the former does not use this specific term). The evidence we have cited so far rather attests to a practical experience of the benefits of music on human behaviour and to its common use in religious rituals that aimed at restoring balance in the human soul (Provenza 2012).

Musical catharsis is better defined by Aristotle in the *Politics*, where the intersections between the medical and religious aspects of the notion are still plainly evident. While discussing musically induced emotions (*pathē*, i.e. 'affections' of the soul which always have a connection with the body since, when we feel them, the body also is affected, cf. III.2),[57] Aristotle gives some details on the cathartic role of music in religious ecstasy (Figure 4):

> For a passion (*pathos*) that strongly affects certain souls occurs in all, varying only in that it may be greater or less: this is the case, for instance, with pity (*eleos*) and fear (*phobos*), and with inspired ecstasy too (*enthousiasmos*). Some people are capable of being entirely possessed by this last disturbance, but we observe that when these people make use of melodies that greatly excite (*exorgiazein*) the soul, out of the resources of sacred melody, they are put right again, just as if they had been given medication (*iatreia*) and purgation (*katharsis*). This must also happen to those who are particularly prone to pity or fear or emotion of any kind, and to others to the extent to which such things affect them: *katharsis* and alleviation (*kouphizesthai*) come to all, and pleasure with them. In the same way invigorating melodies also provides harmless delight for people; and this is why we should allow the contestants who perform the music of the theatre to employ *harmoniai* and melodies of these sorts.
>
> Aristotle, *Politics* 8.7.1342a4–18, transl. Barker 1984

This brief description of musical catharsis, besides helping us to understand the mechanisms underlying its tragic counterpart discussed by Aristotle in the *Poetics*, emphasizes his interest in the physiological changes induced by music.[58] More precisely the term *kouphizesthai* – which is borrowed, as is *katharsis*, from medicine, cf. Ps.-Aristotle, *Problems* 2.22, describing the relief (*kouphizesthai*) from superfluous humours in the human body – indicates the discharge operated by music through a process that cleanses the excitement created by orgiastic melodies by further exposure to the same kind of music.[59] This mechanism is similar to the mechanism thought as operating in modern homeopathic medicine, based on the famous doctrine that 'like cures like' (as stated by the German physician

Samuel Hahnemann, 1755–1843, the founder of modern homeopathy).[60] On the contrary, the Pythagoreans seem to have developed a system functioning in an allopathic way, that is, a system that counteracted diseases with music producing calming effects, opposite to those aroused by exciting music. On this approach, see also Aristoxenus, fr. 122 Wehrli: 'Aristoxenus said that music was introduced because, while it is of the nature of wine to send reeling the bodies and minds of those who indulge in it to the full, music,

Figure 4 Dancing maenad excited by music. Cameo glass medallion (first century CE): New York (USA), Metropolitan Museum 17.194.10.

through its own order and proportion, calms them and leads them into the contrary condition (*eis tēn enantian*)' (transl. Provenza 2012).

The same convergence between medical and musical sources is found in relation to the concept of *harmonia*, i.e. 'harmony', whose modern meaning has departed considerably from the original one.[61] The Greek term *harmonia* comes from the verb *harmozein* ('to fit together', 'to join') and literally means 'fitting together'. In musical contexts, it indicates an attunement of sounds, hence the 'scale' conceived as an organized *structure* of notes, whose ethnic labelling suggests its earlier association with a particular geographical region (IV.3).[62] According to many philosophers and medical writers of the late archaic period (sixth–fifth century BCE), nature and music share the same capacity to beautifully harmonize conflicting opposites: see, e.g., Heraclitus fr. 8 DK ('from differing tones comes the most beautiful *harmonia*') and the Hippocratic *On Regimen* 1.18.1 ('From the same notes come harmonic composition that are not the same, from the sharp and from the deep, which are alike in name but not alike in sound. Those that are the most different make the best concord, those that are least different make the worst').[63] Musical *harmonia* is described as a particularly distinguished example of the structured order of the natural world and the cosmos, where different or opposite elements are connected through a unifying principle: 'Nature in the world-order was fitted together (*harmochthē*, lit. 'harmonized') both out of things which are unlimited and out of things which are limiting, both the world-order as a whole and all the things in it' (Philolaus fr. 1 DK, transl. Barker 2007; the Pythagorean Philolaus is also the first who described the structure of musical octave and called it *harmonia*).[64] Accordingly, since the human body is also composed of opposites, diseases in it arise when its constituents are not governed by a proportioned harmony.[65] The foundation of all the assumptions about music's psychagogic power was the identification of the human soul with *harmonia* (a theory usually ascribed to the Pythagoreans, based on Plato's famous discussion of the *psychē* in the *Phaedo*)[66] or with an entity in search for *harmonia*. The fundamental role of *harmonia* in establishing a good balance between the different parts of the human soul will be then more fully and systematically explored by Plato, who uses music not only as a metaphor to describe the structure of the soul (see especially *Republic* 4.443d–e or *Phaedo* 36.85e–86d),[67] but also as a tool that offers the instruments to create (*Timaeus* 35b–36b) or re-harmonize it (*Timaeus* 80a–c, where the concrete experience of listening to music allows the wise men to reconnect with the original harmonic structure of the World Soul: Barker 2007, 323–6; Pelosi 2010, 190ff. and *passim*). The role of Plato in establishing a long-lasting tradition of inner (i.e. within the soul) and outer (i.e. among celestial bodies) harmony is certainly significant. These ideas, however, were widespread even earlier and became more and more prominent when medical writers and early philosophers with an interest in the nature of the world started to conceive of music as a paradigm of the harmonic integration of opposing elements into the ordered unity of both the human body and the cosmos (II.3).

2

Theoretical Models

1. From *technē* to *epistēmē* (and back)

Most of the surviving documentary evidence on ancient Greek music consists of works on music theory. This corpus of prose texts, extending over a vast period of time (from the late classical to Byzantine periods), reached the Modern Era in manuscripts (see Introduction) mostly containing works on harmonic science, *harmonikē epistēmē*, 'the knowledge concerned with *harmoniai*', i.e. scales. Harmonics was the main theoretical discipline concerned with music; it identifies, classifies and describes the regular and repeated patterns underlying melodic sequences and the rules governing their assemblage in musical compositions (on harmonics and its importance in the wider context of ancient philosophy of science, see Barker 2007).[1] Scientific literature on harmonics was produced for a variety of didactic and scholarly initiatives; it included rather synthetic schooltexts, often provided with practical tools like notational symbols, as well as works of greater intellectual depth (Rocconi 2022a). As a whole, this literature exerted a profound cultural influence on musicians and scholars over nearly two millennia for more than one reason (Gouk 2002). On the one hand, the accurate and rigorous scale-patterns and forms of attunement (the ancient modes and keys) provided the model for new theoretical systems (e.g. the modes of medieval plainchant), leading also to creative attempts to compose new music in what scholars believed to be the Greek style, especially from the late Renaissance onwards (see below). On the other hand, the philosophical credentials of these theoretical texts, especially the mathematically oriented ones (i.e. those displaying a Pythagorean approach, often reinterpreted in the Platonic and Neoplatonic vein), exerted a great fascination on intellectuals of various eras (II.2 and II.3), offering a model also to Christian and Islamic theology (II.4).

The construction and establishment of this theoretical knowledge started quite early in the classical age and subsequently developed in the Hellenistic and post-Hellenistic periods by drawing extensively on – and at the same time deeply influencing – ideas, methods and doctrines in other fields of intellectual study.[2] The two major traditions of thought in ancient harmonics are, broadly speaking, the Pythagorean and the Aristoxenian: the former, which was highly influential throughout the Middle Ages and the early Renaissance, gives a mathematical representation of musical intervals, conceiving them as relationships between quantitative pitches; the latter, which was firmly established by Aristoxenus of Tarentum (*c.* 370/65–? BCE) but whose method had a significant pre-history among musicians themselves (cf. I.1), investigates the components of melody as they appeared in the perceptual realm, with the aim of discovering, by means of reason, the principles governing their combination in music. A distinction between 'mathematical harmonics' (*harmonikē hē te mathēmatikē*) and harmonics 'based on hearing' (*hē kata tēn akoēn*) is already clear-cut in Aristotle's *Posterior Analytics* (1.79a2–6) where, however, these two approaches are still presented as complementary, as he says that the task of those who use perception is to know the fact (*to men oti*) and that of the mathematical scientists to know the reason why (*to de dioti*).[3] The mathematical and empirical branches of music theory were more sharply contrasted only later, under the influence of the debate on the criteria of knowledge that originated with Plato (*c.* 429–347 BCE), and subsequently became the norm in Hellenistic philosophy (Barker 2009). Music as an intellectual discipline continued to animate the philosophical discussions during the first centuries of the Christian era, when it became fundamental for the development of ethical, epistemological and cosmological doctrines (Pelosi and Petrucci 2020).

For many centuries the great mediator of this knowledge to the West was Anicius Manlius Severinus Boethius (*c.* 480–524/6 CE), the Roman philosopher who transmitted the tradition of ancient Greek music theory to the Latin readers of the Middle Ages (Christensen 2018).[4] In his *Fundamentals of Music*, in five books, he adopted a Neopythagorean and Neoplatonic approach (his main sources being Nicomachus of Gerasa (*c.* 60–120 CE) and Claudius Ptolemy (*c.* 100–178 CE)) and classified music and its knowledge into three categories: 'cosmic music' (*musica mundana*, cf. II.3 and 4), which is regarded as the highest kind of music 'discernible especially in those things which are observed in heaven itself'; 'human music' (*musica humana*), the unifying principle for the human being 'that intermingles the elements of the body or holds together the parts of the body in an established order'; 'instrumental music' (*musica instrumentalis*), i.e. produced by various musical instruments 'either by tension, as in strings, or by breath, as in the aulos or those instruments activated by water, or by a certain percussion' (*Fundamentals of Music* 1.2, transl. Bower 1989).[5] Music theory, he says, can become a real science only if it translates sounds and intervals into mathematically measurable quantities; the true *musicus* is neither the performer nor the composer, but the man who has the faculty to *judge* music through a rational approach. The Boethian synthesis – which also includes a critical discussion of the empirical method proposed by Aristoxenus to evaluate consonances, cf. *Fundamentals of Music* 3.1 – entered the canon of medieval education (I.3) and profoundly influenced the development of Western musical thinking, albeit inspiring the so-called *imbroglio des modes* (Chailley 1960), a famous expression coined by the French composer and musicologist Jacques Chailley (1910–99). Indeed, relying solely on Boethius' brief but authoritative explanation of the theory of the modes (as he called them, literally translating the Greek term *tropoi*, i.e. *tonoi* or transposition keys, with the Latin word *modi*), later ninth-century theorists adopted the Greek scale system as a classificatory model for supporting the contemporary modal repertoire and labelled the structures of plainchant with the ancient Greek ethnically based terminology (Bernhard 2007):[6]

> From the species of the consonance of the octave arise what are called *modes*. They are also called *tropes* or *tones*. Tropes are constitutions (i.e. scalar systems) that differ according to highness or lowness throughout entire sequences of pitches. A constitution is, as it were, an entire collection of pitches, brought together within the framework of a consonance such as the octave, the 11th or the double octave. [. . .] If these entire constitutions were made higher or lower in accordance with the species of the consonance of the octave discussed above, this would bring about seven modes, which are named Hypodorian, Hypophrygian, Hypolydian, Dorian, Phrygian, Lydian and Mixolydian.
>
> Boethius, *Fundamentals of Music* 4.15, transl. Bower 1989

This led to the erroneous assumption that the church modes were similar to the Greek modes, encouraging an enduring misunderstanding that lasted until the Renaissance and beyond (Palisca 1985, 280–332; Atkinson 2009).

The search for cultural legitimacy in classical models did not stop even when the mathematical branch of music theory, so strongly supported by Boethius, began to lose its verve among musicians and composers. In the Renaissance, the rediscovery of Greek theorical treatises (see Introduction; cf. Meriani 2016) made it possible to overcome the Boethian mediation and to identify authorities that could provide answers to the new questions about pitch and tuning raised by musicians. Although still praised by many Renaissance musical theorists, in fact, the Pythagorean tuning (made of pure fifths, hence leading to anomalies when playing other intervals derived from these) was not suitable for polyphonic music as it did not make transposition and modulation into any key feasible – therefore the need to search for models that could theoretically support more practical tuning systems, such as the mean-tone or equal temperament, in which all intervals, except the octave, were slightly distorted, i.e. *tempered*. An important figure in this process was Vincenzo Galilei (*c*. 1520–91), the Italian lutenist, composer and theorist who was a member of the Florentine Camerata, a group of intellectuals informally gathering around the figure of the Count Giovanni Bardi (1534–1612) with the ambition to set the artistic trends of their times (Palisca 1989). Galilei had an extensive correspondence with the humanist Girolamo Mei (1519–94), who was a profound connoisseur of ancient Greek musical theory and provider of a significant intellectual impetus to the Camerata (Palisca 1977; Restani 1990). Thanks to Mei, Galilei had access to the work of Aristoxenus, the musical theorist who had carefully avoided arithmetic magnitudes in his analysis of musical intervals;[7] for this reason Galilei identified Aristoxenus as a model of empiricism and introduced his authority in the ongoing discussions about temperament (Palisca 1993; on the importance of 'esperienza' in Galilei's epistemology, see Fix 2019).

In the same period, the ancient musical legacy also provided intellectual justification and validation to new genres that were developing in contemporary performance, such as monody, whose supporters saw in ancient Greek poetry an exemplary model of interpenetration between words and music for expressive purposes,[8] and musical drama, for which the members of the Florentine Camerata found an authoritative archetype in Greek tragedy, whose performers sang on stage.[9] The humanist reinvention of the classical past encouraged scholars throughout the whole of Europe to use Greek theoretical knowledge for musical experiments of various kinds, citing the example of the ancients for justifying their innovations; in this way, they gradually transformed the Greek *epistēmē* back into a *technē*. To name but a few, in 1555 the French philosopher and scholar Pontus de Tyard (1521–1605), member of the French literary circle known as *La Pléiade* (whose intent was to renew French language and literature by imitating ancient Greek poetry), discussed many ancient musical ideas advocating a coherent union of music and poetry; in his work *Solitaire second, ou Prose de la musique* (24–7), he also published a French song by writing it in Greek melodic notation (Wymeersch 2014, 155–62).[10] In France the revival continued in the following decades with the foundation in Paris of the *Académie de poésie et de musique* (1570), which encouraged the composition of Latin and French poetry reproducing the same sort of rhythmical quantity as was observed in classical languages. Examples of this are the *airs mesurés à l'antique*, realized by poets and musicians such as Jean-Antoine de Baïf (1532–89) and Claude Le Jeune (*c*. 1530–1600), although such an experiment, after a brief flowering, died out (Forgács 2021, 51). Similar attempts of imitating the classical meters by setting Horace's odes to music had earlier been made also in the German world, e.g. by the composer and humanist Petrus Tritonius (*c*. 1465–1525: Bergquist and Keyl 2001). Later on, this antiquarian approach influenced the German polymath Athanasius Kircher (1602–80), who in his encyclopaedic work *Musurgia universalis* (*The Universal Musical Art*, 1650) published the (now believed fake) music of Pindar's first *Pythian Ode*, allegedly found by him in a manuscript kept in the Italo-Greek monastery of Santissimo Salvatore at Messina (*Musurgia universalis* 1.541).[11] Almost contextually, in the preface addressed 'to the benevolent reader' of his 1652 *Antiquae musicae autores septem* (*Seven Authors of Ancient Music*, the first modern printed edition, with a Latin translation and commentary, of the most important treatises on Greek music theory), the Danish scholar Marcus Meibom (*c*. 1630–1711) used the ancient melodic notation for setting to music two iambic verses from classical drama, referring to them as examples of the correct application of the ancient Alypian notational symbols.[12]

In Italy too, the impulse given by Greek music theory to the creativity of some composers continued with the advent of the Modern Age. In the seventeenth century, the alleged superiority of musical antiquity led the Florentine theorist Giovanni Battista Doni (1595–1647), heavily influenced by Mei and Galilei, to devote a large part of his scholarly activities to rediscovering and interpreting ancient music theory, especially the Greek tonal system (the main theme of his unpublished and unfinished *Treatise on the Genres and Modes of Music*), and to encourage its revival in modern practice (Palisca and Barbieri 2001).[13] Doni inspired many contemporary musicians and persuaded them to create their own music by using ancient compositional tools (e.g. Pietro Della Valle, 1586–1652, who aimed at restoring the ancient Greek modes and genera in some of his works, e.g. in the *Esthèr* oratorio, 1639: cf. Barbieri 2007). In order to facilitate the performance of Greek melodic models, as he interpreted them, Doni invented experimental musical instruments such as the famous *lyra Barberina*, an amphicordal lyre with strings on the two different sides of its pear-shaped body, so named in honour of Doni's patron Cardinal Francesco Barberini (1597–1679).[14] An earlier invention aimed at a similar purpose had been the *arcicembalo*, a harpsichord equipped with many divided keys which aimed at reproducing the sounds of all three genera of Greek antiquity, realized by the Italian composer and theorist Nicola Vicentino (1511–76), whose new harmonic theories were openly stimulated by Greek antiquity and had an influence on the Flemish composers Cipriano de Rore (1516–65) and Orlande de Lassus (*c.* 1532–94), as far as their use of chromaticism for expressive purposes is concerned.[15] Despite these numerous attempts to influence contemporary music, however, on a practical level the theoretical models of the musical past remained an antiquarian curiosity or were only a vague inspiration for the composers of the period. In the meantime, the growing scientific revolution was bringing attention back to the mathematical branch of Greek music theory, albeit on very different assumptions than in the past (Nolan 2002, 275f.).

2. Music by the numbers

In Greek antiquity, harmonic science was considered a mathematical discipline developed at least as early as Philolaus of Croton (*c.* 470–385 BCE) and Archytas of Tarentum (428–347 BCE), Pythagorean philosophers who conceived of nature as a structured system ordered by (and understood through) number.[16] While the former is the first who describes the structure of the musical octave in mathematical terms (fr. 6a DK, with Huffmann 1993, 145–65; Barker 2007, 263–71), the latter explicitly calls arithmetic and harmonics 'sister sciences' (fr. 1 DK, echoed by Plato, *Republic* 7.530d8: Huffmann 2005, 103–61), shows an interest in acoustics (i.e. the study of material events involved in the production, transmission and perception of sounds: Barker 2007, 305–7)[17] and defines and groups together the three means which were relevant to music: the arithmetic, the geometric and the harmonic, previously called subcontrary (fr. 2 DK: Huffmann 2005, 162–81; Barker 2007, 302f.). The insertion of these means between the numerical values that were assigned to the limiting sounds of the octave (12:6, in ratio 2:1) enabled the generation of the other two 'concords' of Greek music (*symphōniai*, lit. 'consonances', i.e. pleasant combinations of sounds): the fourth (4:3) and the fifth (3:2).[18] The ratios of these three concords are compound by the first four integers (1, 2, 3, 4) whose sum is 10, the so-called *tetraktys* of the decade, which the Pythagoreans regarded as a divine number (Iamblichus, *On the Pythagorean Way of Life* 150). Certainly fictitious is the tale about Pythagoras of Samos (*c.* 585–500 BCE), the mystic, mathematician and philosopher who is said to have discovered the mathematical ratios of musical concords by chance, when hearing some hammers struck by a blacksmith. Multiple sources report that, after the discovery, he verified these proportions on many kinds of vibrating bodies, including the monochord (*kanōn*), i.e. a single string stretched over a sounding board, with a movable bridge dividing the string into two parts in different ratios (Figure 5).[19] There is no allusion, however, to such an instrument before the late fourth century BCE (Creese 2010, esp. 82–4) and the scientific inaccuracy of Pythagoras' experiments was incontrovertibly demonstrated in 1638 by Galileo Galilei (1564–1642: Meriani 1995; Drago 2017).[20] This story rather proves, once again, the Greek habit of identifying a 'first discoverer' (*prōtos heurētes*) for any important phenomenon of their culture (I.1) and attests to the growing legendary aura that surrounded the quasi-magical figure of Pythagoras. The good fortune of this narrative, passed down to the West by Boethius (*Fundamentals of Music* 1.10f.), would last for centuries, consecrating Pythagoras as the authority who first established *true* knowledge of *mousikē* and allowed the interpretation of music and the entire cosmos in mathematical terms (Panti 2020, cf. II.3). Concretely, from the late fourth century BCE onwards, the main matter of dispute between Pythagoreans and Aristoxenians was actually the division of the whole tone (whose ratio is 9:8, i.e. an epitritic/superparticular ratio in which the greater term exceeds the smaller by a simple part of the smaller: $n+1/n$) into any number of equal parts; this process was considered impossible by the former (due to the lack of geometric means between the two terms) and only empirically demonstrated by the latter (see Aristoxenus' famous proof that the fourth consists of two and a half tones in his *Elements of Harmonics* 2.56).[21] String lengths continued to be used by theorists to calculate musical pitches and intervals until the eighteenth century, when they were replaced by frequency values. The quarrel between the two approaches was finally settled by gradually introducing new mathematical tools such as the root extraction – through which intervals of any size could finally be divided into equal

Figure 5 Pythagoras and his musical experiments with numbers. In Franchinus Gaffurius (1451–1522), *Theorica musicae*, Milano 1492.

parts – and by focusing on the physical measurement of vibration frequencies (Rash 2002, 193; Nolan 2002, 278f.).

If the Middle Ages saw the primacy of theory (*musica speculativa*) over practice (*musica practica*), the Renaissance promoted a new alliance between mathematical and practical knowledge in several artistic disciplines: painters developed the linear perspective, architects rediscovered the classical orders and so on.[22] In music, the need to respond to the practical demands of musicians led Gioseffo Zarlino (1517–90), the most important musical theorist of the mid-sixteenth century, to expand the Pythagorean tuning by introducing the *senario* (the set of numbers from one to six, conceived as a conceptual extension of the ancient *tetraktys*), whose ratios explained not only the consonances recognized by the ancients – octave, fifth and fourth – but also the major and minor thirds (5:4, 6:5) and sixths (5:3, 8:5, the number 8 being included only potentially in the *senario*),[23] i.e. intervals which were widely used in contemporary polyphony. Zarlino reformed the ancient quantitative tradition from within by appealing to another Greek authority: Claudius Ptolemy, author of a treatise on harmonics in three books (Barker 1989, 270–391). The model of the 'syntonic diatonic' scale which Ptolemy had praised in his *Harmonics* (1.15), because it was entirely made up of superparticular ratios, met Zarlino's needs and was thus adjusted to the modern octave scale (in descending order): 9:8, 10:9, 16:15, 9:8, 10:9, 9:8, 16:15 (*Le istitutioni harmoniche*, Venice 1558, 2.39).[24] By displaying a 'just' intonation, this scale combined theory with practice; its intervals were expressed by ratios between simple whole numbers – hence mathematically acceptable – but their tuning could also produce pleasant thirds and sixths, which would have been dissonant, instead, in the Pythagorean diatonic scale (Gozza 2000, 7–9; Palisca 2001a; cf. Lindley 2001).[25]

Zarlino's advocacy of a mathematical explanation for consonances soon became outdated. Yet the numerological models remained popular in later centuries, not only among theorists but also among musicians, as shown by the various usages of numbers by twentieth-century composers who operated in the context of a rapidly changing harmonic language, e.g. Arnold Schoenberg (1874–1951) and Iannis

Xenakis (1922–2001). The former was the pioneer, in the 1920s, of the twelve-tone *serialism* as a method of composing music that arranges the twelve notes of the chromatic scale in a fixed-order series, making them the basis on which to build up a melody. The latter was founder of the *Equipe de mathématique et automatique musicales* (1966), which led to the creation of a computerized music composition system (Maor 2018).[26] The epistemological shift from the idea of *music as a science* to *music as an art* (i.e. from *epistēmē* to *technē*) that occurred in the Age of the Enlightenment completely redesigned the ancient classification of scholarly disciplines, definitively detaching music from the quadrivial model and inserting it within the system of 'fine arts' (Kristeller 1981, 163–227). One aspect, however, of the Pythagorean-Platonic intellectual tradition on music did continue to exert a profound influence on the conceptual universe of both scholars and musicians: the doctrine of world harmony.

3. Cosmic ideals

In 1989–90, the French musician Gérard H. Grisey (1946–98) composed *Le Noir de l'Étoile*, for six percussionists, magnetic tape and astronomic signals emitted by pulsars (Grisey 1990). The first performance of this piece took place in Brussels (Belgium) on 16 March 1991; the periodic impulses of these neutron stars, whose radio waves were picked up and amplified by a loudspeaker, were transmitted directly to the concert hall and gradually inserted within the rhythmic texture performed by the percussionists (i.e. the famous group *Les Percussions de Strasbourg*) all positioned around the audience, arousing a great emotional reaction in the public.[27] Exactly four hundred years earlier (1589), the audience of the most spectacular event of the end of the sixteenth century, i.e. the magnificent entertainments for the wedding of Ferdinando de' Medici and

Christine of Lorraine in Florence, was amazed by the *intermedi* celebrating the power of ancient music through mythological tales, whose first episode was dedicated to 'The Harmony of the Spheres' (Palisca 1985, 187–90).[28] The goddess Harmonia, represented as a woman (Figure 6), descended from heaven while a chorus of Sirens used their song to move the celestial spheres, which revolved around Necessity and her three daughters, the Fates, who were placed at the centre of the stage. They all praised the wedding couple, performing 'such a sweet melody [...] that it seems deriving from Paradise' (Bastiano de' Rossi, *Description of the apparatus and the 'intermedi' made for the comedy performed in Florence at the wedding of Serenissimi Don Ferdinando Medici, and Madama Cristina di Loreno, Grand Dukes of Tuscany*, Florence 1589, 20).[29] These outstanding events are only two of the many variations on the theme of cosmic harmony in the history of Western music.

Figure 6 The goddess Harmonia descends to earth. Design by the architect and theatrical designer Bernardo Buontalenti (1531–1608) for the first *intermedio* of *La Pellegrina* (Florence 1589).

The belief in a sounding universe governed by mathematical laws notoriously originated in Greek antiquity, with parallels in Babylonian, Jewish and Islamic culture (Haar 1961; Haar 2001; Shiloah 2018). The Pythagoreans are usually credited with the genesis of this idea,[30] which is, however, attested for the first time in two Platonic dialogues: the *Republic* and the *Timaeus*.[31] In the *Republic* (10.617b–c), while recounting the post-mortem experience of a soldier named Er (who, during his journey in the afterworld, could admire the structure of the entire cosmos), Plato describes the universe as a set of eight concentric and rotating rings, on whose surfaces there is an equal number of singing Sirens, each of them uttering a sound of different pitch (Viltanioti 2015); from all these sounds, 'the concord of a single harmony is made' (*mian harmonian xymphōnein*, 617b8, with Pelosi 2018). Three Fates sit around and sing to (*hymnein pros*) the *harmonia* of the Sirens (probably to be conceived as the octave framework on which the song of the Fates is based: Barker 1989, 58 n. 11).[32] In the cosmogony of the *Timaeus* (35a–36d), Plato portrays a divinely created universe, whose Craftsman builds the World Soul (that is, the entity which animates and gives order to the living cosmos: Wilberding 2021) by applying mathematical principles to a mixed substance (Brisson 2021). He thus obtains an arrangement of geometric lengths (*diastēmata*, the same Greek word used to indicate the musical 'intervals': Rocconi 2003, 73) corresponding to an enormous Pythagorean scale – spanning four octaves and a major sixth – organized into perfect fifths and fourths, the latter in turn divided into diatonic tetrachords (Barker 2007, 318–23).[33] Later in the dialogue, we are told that such a divine *harmonia* is mimetically reproduced in mortal movements generating high- and low-pitched sounds, whose perception provides pleasure (*hēdonē*) to people of poor understanding and delight (*euphrosynē*) to those of good understanding (80b). This is the reason why, by listening to music, the human soul may tune itself with cosmic harmony and restore its own balance, if compromised (47c–e, with Pelosi 2010, 65–9 and 73–80). Since antiquity, these two texts have been read together by Plato's most influential interpreters, who merged the two conceptually interconnected (but originally distinct) notions of *music of the spheres* and *world harmony* into a single idea that profoundly shaped Western thought for the centuries to come. Indeed, the idea of a cosmos governed by a musical *harmonia,* rooted in well-established mathematical relationships, helped philosophy, theology and music theory of different historical periods, from Antiquity up to early Modern Era, to bring order and meaning to their worlds, also providing modern science with the model of a mathematical universe that still fascinates us.

Aristotle notoriously rejected the idea of a sonorous universe by arguing that, if cosmic sounds existed, we would perceive their noise and would be affected by their immense force (*On the Heavens* 2.9.290b–291a). Despite this illustrious opponent, the notion of world harmony circulated widely in late antiquity thanks to the numerous commentaries on Plato's *Timaeus:*[34] it was revived by Cicero (106–43 BCE) in the *Dream of Scipio* (made popular especially by its commentator Macrobius, *c.* 385–430 CE, see his *Commentary on the Dream of Scipio*), by Neoplatonic theorists such as Nicomachus (*Manual of Harmonics* ch. 3) and Boethius (whose idea of *musica mundana* became a recurring topos in the Middle Ages),[35] and by a great number of medieval authors (Hicks 2017). The idea was echoed by the poet Dante Alighieri (1265–1321) who, in spite of his close adherence to Aristotelianism, in the *Paradise* mentions 'the harmony which Thou (sc. the God) attunest and modulatest' (1.78, the whole passage is 1.76–84), interpreting celestial music as an intellectual action that instils desire for, and allows access to, the harmony of divine perfection. See especially *Paradise* 1.82–4: 'The novelty of the sound and the great light kindled in me a desire concerning their cause, never before felt with such acuteness' (transl. Norton 1892).[36] As a matter of fact, one of the most debated aspects of world harmony concerns the concrete possibility, for cosmic music, to produce *real* sounds that can be perceived with the senses by human beings, at least by those who are worthy of it (e.g. Pythagoras, see Iamblichus, *On the Pythagorean Way of Life* 65: 'he alone could hear and understand [...] the universal harmony and concord of the spheres, and the stars moving through them, which sound a tune fuller and more intense than any mortal ones', transl. Dillon and Hershbell 1991).[37] Alternative interpretations, such as Dante's, rather explained this music as a pure intellectual act, through which men can grasp an intelligible realm beyond the senses and understand the harmonic relationships regulating the ordered structure of the universe.[38] Moreover, the psychagogic implications of the similarities, suggested in the *Timaeus*, between the harmony of heavenly music and the harmony of the human soul have often been used to explain the emotional power of music on human beings (III.2), for instance by Renaissance Neoplatonic physicians such as the Florentine humanist Marsilio Ficino (1433–99). Ficino adapted Plato's ideas on the connection between the World Soul and the human soul to the new intellectual and artistic context in which he lived. By singing the Orphic hymns to the accompaniment of his *lyra orphica* (most probably a *lira da braccio*, a bowed string instrument typical of the Renaissance), he attempted to revitalize for therapeutic purposes the magic singing of Orpheus, who – he believed – was initiated, like Pythagoras and Plato, into the secrets of the cosmos and could hence act as an intermediary between the music of the spheres and its recreation in the sensible world (Ficino, *Timaeus Commentary* 31 and 33; *Platonic Theology* 4.1.28; with Walker 1958, 19f.; Prins 2015, 119–213; Vanhaelen 2018).[39] Ficino's *Three Books on Life* (first circulated in manuscript, then published in 1489) was printed in over thirty editions and several vernacular translations; with its focus on the interconnection between musical modes, bodily temperaments and planetary harmonies, this work became the paradigmatic text for discussions of music's effects on human body until the seventeenth century (Gouk 2002, 226; see also III.2).

The theme of cosmic harmony continued to be transformed and adapted to new scientific, intellectual and artistic contexts throughout history, combining – each time in different order and proportions – poetic imagination with mathematical models and religious feelings, all ingredients that were already present at the origin of its tradition, i.e. in Platonic writings (Walker 2000, 75). Although in antiquity and the Middle Ages this idea was clearly connected to the Ptolemaic model of the universe, with Earth at the centre, the harmony of the spheres continued to hold a fascination long after the Ptolemaic system was replaced by a different cosmological model: the Copernican, i.e. heliocentric, model. Constructively relying on the idea of a system of planets and stars bound by a harmony of proportionate distances and speeds, Johannes Kepler (1571–1630) used geometry and musical harmony to explain the structure of the universe (Walker 1967; Dickreiter 2000; Gozza 2000, 42–9; Gouk 2002, 233–5). After having determined the elliptical, not circular, orbit of the planets and the law of motion of each of them (which varies in relation to the distance from one of the two foci of the rotation of the ellipse), in *The Harmony of the World* (*Harmonices mundi*, Linz 1619) Kepler formulated his famous third planetary law, also called 'harmonic law', according to which a planet's orbital period is proportional to the size of its orbit. He discovers that it is the speeds, not the distances, of the planets that form the physical basis of celestial music. The (polyphonic) harmonies produced by the different planets can hence be found in the values of the minimum and maximum orbital speeds of each of them. Such an investigation into the harmony of the spheres, although still imbued with religious feelings (Kepler saw in the universe the imprint of God acting as a geometer, on the ancient Platonic model),[40] opened the doors to modern science, providing scientists with the conceptual tools for solving the astronomical problem of defining the relationships between the times of revolution, on the one hand, and the distances of the planets, on the other. After Kepler, the English mathematician Isaac Newton (1642–1727) also assigned scientific value to cosmic music by interpreting the harmony of the spheres as a symbolic expression of his theory of universal gravitation (Gozza 2000, 50; Gouk 2002, 235–9).

In September 2015, the harmony of the spheres made headlines again; the Laser Interferometer Gravitational-Wave Observatory (LIGO) finally detected the gravitational wave signals that had been predicted by Albert Einstein in the early twentieth century (Bartusiak 2020) and presented them, shortly thereafter (11 February 2016), to the public as the *cosmic song* that resonates throughout the universe.[41] The long journey that started in early classical Greece and has spanned more than two millennia seems not to have reached its end.

4. In the praise of God

Among the reinterpretations of cosmic harmony, few have the imaginative power of the 'monochord of the world' (*monochordum mundi*) elaborated by Robert Fludd (1574–1637), an English physician and polymath with interests in cosmology and occult philosophies, author of *The Metaphysical, Physical, and Technical History of the Two Worlds, namely the Major and the Minor* (Oppenheim 1617–19, in two volumes: Ammann 1967; Giles 2016; Guariento 2018). Fludd's cosmic monochord extended from the highest to the lowest level of creation, i.e. the macrocosm of the universe, correlating the sounds of the Boethian two-octaves scale with the spheres of elements, planets and angels (on the adherence of Fludd's form of exposition to the Boethian text, see Giles 2016, 134). This celestial instrument was plucked by the divine hand of a God/Player (*Pulsator monochordi*) who, through it, created harmony in the material world, i.e. the microcosm of man.[42] In the history of Western thought, indeed, the symmetries and harmonies displayed by the music of the spheres have often been read as the reflection of a divine project, with the result of reconciling the Platonic Craftsman with the God of the various monotheisms, which represented him as the *geometer* of the world we are living in (II.3). This has certainly favoured the diffusion in Christian literature of the idea of world harmony which, together with other musical themes and images resulting from the synthesis of Christian and pagan cultures, widely circulated throughout the Middle Ages and beyond (as, e.g., the image of Christ/Orpheus, on which see Skeris 1976). Contrary to what happened in the other examples discussed so far, however, this process of assimilation was not a means for legitimizing new ideas through their supposed derivation from the great models of the past, as Christian writers were generally very critical of pagan culture and they would never openly claim it as a model. It rather worked as a strategy of appropriation that, by remodelling old ideas, helped these authors define their own identity and demonstrate the excellence of their religious belief, while at the same time creating an undeclared continuity with the ancients and thus making the transition smoother (Pelosi 2020a).

Christian culture reshaped the idea of cosmic music in many different ways. The theme passed to the Church Fathers through Philo of Alexandria (*c.* 20 BCE–45 CE), a Hellenistic Jewish thinker who formulated his own concept of universal harmony (*On Flight and Finding* 112) and interpreted the harmony of the spheres as a song of praise raised to God by 'the sun and moon and the most sacred choir of the other stars', in which the prophet Moses also actively participated (*On the Virtues* 72–5, with Lévy 2020, esp. 35ff.). The first Christian writer to adopt this image was the theologian Clement of Alexandria (*c.* 150–215 CE). In the opening chapter of his *Exhortation to the Greeks* (1.5.1–4), he presents the Word of Christ, i.e. his redeeming and truthful message, as the 'New Song' that gives order and harmony to the entire universe and described Christ as a divine musical *tuner*,[43] also projecting the harmonious arrangement of the cosmos onto the constitutive elements of human beings (Raffa 2016; Kramarz 2018; Pelosi 2020a, 156–71).[44] Shortly afterwards, the Christian scholar Origen of Alexandria (*c.* 184–253 CE) used the same image as Philo – i.e. the 'sacred choir' quoted above – when describing the 'divine choir' of the sun, moon, stars and all the heavenly host, together with just men, who sing hymns of praise to God and His only-begotten Son (*Against Celsus* 8.67, with Pelosi 2020a, 171–7). In later Christian sources, heavenly sounds are usually said to be produced by angels (e.g. Dante, *Paradise* 31.130–5). This supposedly happened on the basis of the apocryphal text of the Old Testament known as *The Second Book of Enoch* (or *The Book of the Secrets of Enoch*, nowadays preserved only in Church Slavonic) which, together with other fragmentary literature once circulating under the name of Enoch, had wide dissemination among Christian writers for several centuries:

> And there are three hundred angels very glorious, who keep the garden and with never ceasing voices and blessed singing, they serve the Lord every day.
>
> In the middle of the heavens, I saw an armed host serving the Lord with cymbals, and organs, and unceasing voice. I was delighted at hearing it.
>
> *The Book of the Secrets of Enoch* 9.1 and 17.1,
> transl. Morfill and Charles 1896[45]

At the dawn of the Middle Ages, when music as a mathematical discipline had become an expression of the divine order, the theologian and philosopher Augustine of Hippo (354–430 CE) presented a universe based on the notion of *numerus* ('rhythm'), the key to understanding its ordered structure (Wiskus 2015; Michon 2016). According to Augustine, the *numerus* is the ontological root of finite beauty (Augustine, *On Music* 6.13.38), i.e. a polysemic term embracing a wide range of meanings, under whose umbrella sensible and intelligible realities appear unified: 'Rhythm has its principle in the One. It derives its beauty from regularity and similitude, its arrangement from order' (*On Music* 6.17.56, transl. Michon 2016). His doctrines were heavily influenced by Neoplatonism and, at the same time, based on the principle that material reality is no longer an obstacle but rather a step towards the ascent to incorporeal realities. With these assumptions, Augustine conceives of the world harmony, i.e. 'the beauty of the whole world' (*universi saeculi pulchritudo*), in terms of *time* (Spitzer 1944, esp. 432ff.; Spitzer 1945).[46] In his view, the world is like a great song performed by a God-musician (*velut magnum carmen cuiusdam ineffabilis modulatoris*), creator and ruler of the universe (*sicut creator, ita moderator*, see *On Music* 6.17.57), openly described as *faber*, i.e. a 'craftsman':

> As *the immutable creator and governor of mutable things*, he knows better than a human being what at a particular time he ought to give, add, remove, subtract, increase, or decrease *until the beauty of the whole world*, whose parts are those things that are suited for their own times, *is played out like a great song of a certain ineffable artist* [. . .].
>
> Augustine, *Letter* 138.5, transl. Teske 1990, italics mine

By giving order to the times (*dispositor temporum*), God is not only the source of order and beauty in the universe. He becomes *composer* himself of such a cosmic musical harmony:

> Since I would also say this of the leaf of a tree and of the number of our hairs, how much more do I say this of the birth and death of a human being, whose temporal life does not extend shorter or longer than *God, who gives order to the times* (*Deus dispositor temporum*), *knows harmonizes with the melody of the universe* (*novit universitatis moderamini consonare*)!
>
> Augustine, *Letter* 166.13, transl. Teske 2004, italics mine

Aesthetic Issues

1. Senses and sensibilities

In the history of Western aesthetics, classical Greece has often embodied an ideal of beauty. This may appear as a truism when we talk about visual arts, especially sculpture; but the path outlined in the previous chapters makes clear that Greek music (or, better, *mousikē*) was frequently seen as an ideal to strive for and to return to cyclically or, alternatively, as a precedent to overcome. If we turn our attention to the reflections of the ancients on the ways in which human beings responded emotionally and cognitively to artistic experiences and then converged these perceptions into evaluations of some kind (appreciation or criticism), *mousikē* stands out for being the most widely discussed kind of art(s), sometimes in a highly polemical way. The purpose of this chapter is to summarize the main issues around which musical aesthetic thought originated and developed throughout antiquity and to show what themes among them became significant in the following centuries, even without any direct allusion to the Greek legacy.

I will begin by retracing the crucial debate between sense perception and reason which was the basis for all ancient reasoning on *mousikē*, both in the context of speculations in harmonic science (II.1) and throughout the discussions on the criteria for *judging* music. The so-called *cognitive turn* that, for some years, has affected numerous disciplines within the humanities, especially reflections on art, has enabled scholars in the field to profit from the basic framework, methodology and conceptual apparatus developed by neuroscientists and to explore the neural basis of aesthetic experience (see, e.g., Starr 2013).[1] This has led to a new field of experimental science called neuroaesthetics (for the coinage of the term, see Zeki 1997, 1999 and 2001), whose principles can be fruitfully applied to antiquity (Meineck, Short and Devereaux 2018), albeit with necessary caution, as we have no unmediated access to the raw scientific data of the past. It must be said that the Greeks' endorsement of a cognitively oriented approach to the appreciation (or criticism) of music has never completely overshadowed the contribution of sensory perception. The role of the senses was widely discussed not only in philosophical writings, but it also left significant traces in the language with which the poets described sound phenomena. To give just one example, the metaphors originally underlying what later became the qualifying adjectives of the pitch spectrum, *oxys* and *barys* (i.e. 'high-' and 'low-pitched', lit. 'sharp' and 'heavy', said of material objects), were recurrent in Homeric poetry to describe the impact of sounds, conceived as bodies, on their producers or perceivers (Rocconi 2003, 54–8). See, for instance, the formulas 'groaning heavily' (*bary stenachōn*), which denotes a heaviness or emotional pain in the heart of a mourner, or 'lamenting shrill'/'with a shrill cry' (*oxy kōkysasa*), suggesting that the crying strikes the hearer like a pointed arrow (on laments in Greek funerary context cf. Figure 7).[2] A recent book by James Porter (2010) has provocatively brought attention back to matter and sensation as important foundations of Greek aesthetic thought, attempting to redefine the relationship between materialism and formalism in a more dynamic way, i.e. not considering them as mutually opposed but connected to the same *experience* of art (cf. Peponi 2012). Indeed, the etymological root of the word *aesthetics*, created by Alexander Baumgarten in the mid-eighteenth century (cf. his *Aesthetica* in two vols, 1750–58) and, shortly after, formalized by Immanuel Kant (see especially his *Critique of Judgment*, published in 1790), points to

Figure 7 Women lamenting during a *prothesis* (i.e. 'laying out of a dead'). Attic black-figure funerary plaque (*c.* 520–510 BCE): New York (USA), Metropolitan Museum 54.11.5.

aisthēsis, i.e. 'perception' as the first medium through which we sense artworks. This is why a sensory approach to cultural history has recently been so successful in many branches of scholarship, including Classical Studies (see, e.g., Toner 2016; Butler and Nooter 2018). Let us now have a closer look at some important Greek texts discussing music that exemplify the liveliness of this debate in antiquity.

We cannot but begin with Plato, the fiercest opponent of a sensory approach to *mousikē* (cf. especially *Republic* 7.530c–531c, quoted in ch. II n. 32), who nevertheless shows sometimes unexpected interest in this issue (on music and sensation in Plato, see especially Gurd 2019, chs 1–3). In one of the dialogues we have already mentioned in chapter one, i.e. the *Laws*, Plato examines who should be entrusted with the role of judge of 'what is beautiful' in music (*to kalon*, see III.4) – in his view, the oldest and most educated people in the city – and what are the criteria on which to base their judgment (Bartels 2012; Rocconi 2012). The basic assumption of this reasoning is the mimetic character of music, reaffirmed by Plato whenever he writes about *mousikē*, see, e.g., *Republic* 3.399a–401a and *Laws* 2.668a: 'All music is likeness-making and mimetic' (transl. Barker 1984). As in any other art, in fact, music produces things *in the likeness* of other things, as if to say it imitates or represents emotions, characters and even actions of human beings of a particular kind (III.3). According to Plato, the three qualifications that anyone who is to judge intelligently (*emphrona*) must have are the following: first, he must know 'what' the original of such an imitation is (*ho te esti*); secondly, how 'correctly' (*orthōs*) that particular representation is made; thirdly, how 'well' (*eu*) it is made in words, melodies and rhythms (*Laws* 2.667b–671a).[3] Especially when Plato discusses the correctness (*orthotēs*) of imitation, the explicit reference is to the technical accuracy and precision of the artists in realizing the correspondence to the model (668d); in the musical field, this means an appropriate assemblage of the melodic and rhythmic elements that make up the music (669c–d, cf. *Laws* 7.802a–e). In order to evaluate such a correctness, it is hence essential that those judging musical compositions 'have both acute perception (*euaisthētōs echein*) and understanding (*gignōskein*) of rhythms and scales' (670b: no mention is made here to the words, i.e. the *logos*). This proves that the interplay between these two faculties, perception and cognitive capacity, becomes necessary when dealing with sensible objects, as in the case of the music that people experience in everyday life.[4] To put it another way, even if the ultimate goal of his third (and highest) level of judgment goes beyond the pleasant perception of *mousikē* – grounded in its sensuous appeal (654a)[5] – and rather deals with its ethical dimension, Plato considers the coherence between form and content an essential property of works of art and he regards its accurate assessment a fundamental phase of the whole evaluation process.

The most explicit discussion of the criteria involved in musical judgment may be read in the writings of Aristoxenus of Tarentum (*c.* 370/65–? BCE), whose defence of perception was strongly influenced by his Aristotelian background and has been widely recognized, and often criticized, by those who later discussed his work in the field of harmonics (see esp. II.1). According to him, musical phenomena must be interpreted 'according to the representation of perception' (*kata tēn tēs aisthēseōs phantasian*),[6] since it is from the synthesis of many different sensorial experiences that we obtain a more comprehensive and coherent impression of musical phenomena (here he is talking about the musical melody traveling through the dimension of pitch, on which see Barker 2007, 140–50).[7] The *kritikē dynamis*, i.e. the business of forming judgments of any kind about a piece of music, relies on both perception and reason (coadiuvated by the faculty of memory);[8] but, in order to evaluate how melodic and rhythmic elements are assembled together, these two faculties must run along together (*homodromein*).[9] This is a very intriguing insight; nowadays we are fully aware that the audible information received through our sensory receptors are organized into meaningful items (i.e. recognized as *musical*) only thanks to our brain. In recent years the process of parsing the complex acoustic data that reach our ears into auditory perceptual objects, hence coming to represent melodies or rhythmical patterns, found a theoretical framework in the *auditory scene analysis* (ASA), an expanding research field in psychoacoustics (Bregman 1994).

According to Aristoxenus, the two final objects of any critical judgment on music are composition (*poiēma*) and its performance/interpretation (*hermēneia*): 'some of the things which are objects of our judgment are ends in themselves, while others are not. An individual composition is such an end, a piece which is sung, for instance, or one played on the aulos [. . .] and so is the performance of any of these, the playing on the aulos, the singing, etc.' (Ps.-Plutarch,

On Music 36.1144d, transl. Barker 1984). It is precisely when the discussion moves to the performer's interpretation of a specific piece of music that Aristoxenus mentions its aesthetic character (*ēthos*), describing it as capable of *expressing* (and *not* imitating, cf. III.3) specific emotions:

> Over and above these matters and all others like them, judgment will be passed on the character (*ēthos*) of the performance, to decide whether the performer's interpretation is appropriate (*oikeion*) to the composition that was entrusted to him, and which he was seeking to execute and interpret. The same applies to the emotions expressed (*pathōn* [. . .] *sēmainomenōn*)[10] in compositions through the art which is proper to composers.[11]
>
> Ps.-Plutarch, *On Music* 36.1144e, transl. Barker 1984

Anyone who is to distinguish the appropriate (*to oikeion*) and the inappropriate (*to allotrion*) in music must identify the *ēthos* at which the composition is aiming and the elements from which the composition has been put together (i.e. note, duration and syllable, see *On Music* 34.1143d).[12] This is why any complete musician and critic (*teleos mousikos* and *kritikos*, cf. *On Music* 36.1144c–d)[13] must base, albeit not limit, his theoretical understanding of musical phenomena on a perception as accurate as possible: 'accuracy of perception stands out just about first in order of importance, since if he (sc. the student of music) perceives badly it is impossible for him to give a good account of the things which he does not perceive at all' (*Elements of Harmonics* 33.21–6, transl. Barker 1989). But, in order to be accurate, perception requires training (*syngymnasia*) directed towards a grasp of melody and rhythm (*On Music* 36.1144c), a practice that in some cases may be challenging, as in the case of the perception of enharmonic melodies; we become accustomed to them at last, with difficulty and through much hard work (*Elements of Harmonics* 19.27f.).[14] This possibility for perception to be *trainable* suggests that, in order for it to become cognitively useful, it must be enriched with a sort of background knowledge that allows any musically educated listener to *grasp* (before conceptually recognizing) enharmonic or chromatic intervals, that is, to identify sounds as relations of pitches and not as pure quantities. See *Elements of Harmonics* 33.32–4, where Aristoxenus explicitly states that differences of genera are, first of all, *perceive*d by the listeners: 'we perceive (*aisthanometha*) differences of genera when the bounding notes remain fixed while the intermediate ones change' (cf. Barker 1991, esp. 210–12).[15] Therefore Aristoxenus considers perception not theoretically neutral but *dynamic*, exactly like music (cf. *Elements of Harmonics* 38.31f., quoted at n. 8; on the dynamic character of music, see also 48.14–18, quoted at n. 27). The same idea has been extensively discussed in recent years in the field of cognitive psychology. According to the so-called New Look theory – a twentieth-century theory originating in the US that developed an innovative approach to the study of perception, no longer seen as a self-sufficient process but dependent on beliefs and expectations – perception is not simply a *response* dependent on a stimulus, but something that involves mental (albeit unconscious) processing.[16]

The debate between perception and reason remained central in any theoretical discussion on music from the Hellenistic age to Late Antiquity, especially in the context of harmonic science: see the disputes between Pythagoreans and Aristoxenians (already mentioned in II.1), which also involved nuances and intermediate positions on both sides (Barker 2009). The growing importance of the mathematical conception of music progressively obscured the relevance of a *sensorial* approach to it which, however, persisted within the reflections on its pedagogical and ethical value intertwining with the controversies over its mimetic power, that is, on the idea that *mousikē* can convey extra-musical content (III.3). In this regard, particularly interesting is the debate between Stoic and Epicurean philosophers, partially preserved in some surviving fragments of the treatise *On Music* by the Epicurean Philodemus of Gadara (*c.* 110–35 BCE). In this text

Philodemus attacks the view of the Stoic Diogenes of Babylon (*c.* 230–150 BCE), who believed that we experience music through a 'knowing' or 'cognitive perception' (*epistēmonikē aisthēsis*), that is a scientific form of sensation that can tell us 'what is in harmony and what is not' (*On Music* 4, col. 34.2–8, cf. col. 115.26–35: on the notion of 'knowing perception', see now Klavan 2019). In Philodemus' view, music is not imitative and has no semantic content at all, therefore it cannot have any ethically beneficial effects on human beings. The pleasure it arouses is *unnecessary* and exclusively sensual. As a consequence, the Epicurean philosopher deprives sensation of any cognitive significance and proposes a notion of perception which is nothing more than an automatic response to a sensorial stimulus (Barker 2001; Pelosi 2020b).

2. Music and emotions

Emotions are key to any aesthetic experience. The ancient Greek term that comes closest to our idea of 'emotion' is *pathos*, from *paschein* (i.e. 'to suffer', 'to experience'), whose use in this sense seems to have been a relatively late development, namely after 420s BCE (Harris 2001, 84; Singer 2022). Still after that date, the meaning of the term *pathos* only partially overlaps with its modern counterpart; scholars with a historical approach to the topic have frequently pointed out how the experiences we choose to label as emotions mostly depend on the culture (Konstan 2006, 1–40; Cairns 2019, 1–5). Indeed, in the last few decades, the humanities and social sciences have entered the lively scientific debate on emotions by challenging and problematizing some of the shared assumptions of modern psychology and evolutionary theory, such as the universalist approach to emotions proposed by Charles Darwin (*The Expression of the Emotions in Man and Animals*, London 1872) and recently reaffirmed by the American psychologist Paul Ekman and other cognitive scientists,[17] which are to be considered potentially misleading when the goal is a *history* of emotions (Rosenwein 2010). Hence the need has arisen to overcome the idea of emotions as pure biological entities and to adopt key concepts like emotional community and emotional culture from social constructionism, contextualizing them in historical dimensions and focusing on the language and thought patterns through which we (and ancient sources) discuss emotions (Stearns and Stearns 1985; Rosenwein 2002; Rosenwein 2006).

Despite the tendencies of a significant part of modern scholarship to separate the cognitive from the embodied approach to emotions, we know that the Greeks considered the emotional states determined by an interaction of cognitive factors with a state of physiological arousal (see I.4, esp. n. 57; for the opposite trend, see below). Emotions are reactions to impinging events (*locus classicus* for their discussion is Book 2 of Aristotle's *The Art of Rhetoric*, cf. IV.4) usually accompanied by physical reactions, as we are told by several sources, from the Hippocratic medical writings – where emotions are most often treated as an extension of the body – to Peripatetic evidence: 'that the body suffers sympathetically (*sympaschon*) with affections (*pathēmasi*) of the soul is evident in love, fear, grief and pleasure' (Ps.-Aristotle, *Physiognomics* 805a6–9, transl. Hett 1936).[18] When describing the emotional response to music, the ancients describe it at first as an *embodied* experience that, before affecting cognitive faculties, engages sensory-motor processes (see Figure 4): 'virtually every young creature is incapable of keeping still with either its body or its voice, but is always trying to move and make sounds, leaping and skipping as though dancing and sporting with pleasure, and uttering noises of every kind' (Plato, *Laws* 2.653d–e, transl. Barker 1984).[19] The most emblematic account of an exceptionally strong reaction to music caused by precognitive affective appraisals (i.e. unmediated by any cognitive mechanism) is given in a famous tale told by many sources, both Greek and Latin, in connection with Pythagoras of Samos (*c.* 585–500 BCE). According to the most famous version of this story narrated by Iamblichus of Chalcis (*c.* 245–325 CE) in his *On the Pythagorean Way of Life* 112, Pythagoras managed to calm the frenzy of a youth from Tauromenium (modern Taormina, in Sicily), who had previously been inflamed and excited by a Phrygian melody played by a pipe-player, simply by asking the musician to switch to the libation tune (i.e., the *spondeion*, a melody for solo aulos), which was rhythmically slower and used a Dorian, instead of a Phrygian, melody.[20]

Overall, ancient evidence deals extensively with the theme of music and emotions. Greek discussions on the topic would influence to a large extent – especially in the Baroque period – the so-called *theory of the affects* or *Affektenlehre*, from the term used by German musicologists in the twentieth century to describe the great emphasis placed by seventeenth- and eighteenth-century composers on the capacity of music to arouse different emotional responses from their audience. This idea was also supported by important theorists such as René Descartes (1596–1650), Athanasius Kircher (1602–80) and Johann Mattheson (1681–1764).[21] The main interest of ancient Greek texts concerns two different, but closely related, aspects: on the one hand the elicitation of emotions in human beings through specific musical components, such as scales, rhythms or genres of compositions, which some authors (e.g. Plato) attempt to channel into socially desirable ends; on the other hand the capacity of music to represent and/or express human emotions (for an overview, see Rocconi 2019a; Pelosi 2020). I will now give some examples of the Greeks' contribution to a few issues on which modern scholarly debate has more extensively focused: some of the mechanisms that modern scientists consider responsible for arousing musical emotions (i.e. *contagion* and *empathy*) and the *expressiveness* of music.[22]

As we have repeatedly pointed out in Chapter 1, the Greek experience of *mousikē* was always collective and, due to the lack of recording tools, necessarily occurring in live performances (Butler 2015). The frequent and numerous participatory contexts in which ancient people performed and listened to music involved the body and movement more often than in modern experiences (where a solitary and intellectualized listening tends to prevail) and make the phenomenon of the so-called *emotional contagion* quite probable. With this expression modern scholars indicate the social phenomenon of shared emotional expression and synchronization of movements and vocalizations occurring outside of conscious awareness (Hatfield, Cacioppo and Rapson 1994; Hatfield, Rapson and Le 2009; Hatfield, Carpenter and Rapson 2014). This echoing or mirroring emotional response provoked by music is mentioned only occasionally in ancient Greek sources but, when it does, interesting details are given. In some Peripatetic sources, for instance, we are provided with possible explanations for the process of *sympathein*, i.e. 'feeling with' – corresponding to what we today call empathy – that spontaneously occurs between the performer and the perceiver:[23]

Why do people listen with more pleasure to people singing melodies they happen to know beforehand, than if they do not know them? [...] is it *because the listener is sympathetic (sympathēs) with the one singing what is recognized? For he sings it with him.* And everyone enjoys singing who is not obliged to do this.

Ps.-Aristotle, *Problems* 19.40, transl. Mayhew 2011, italics mine

Why do people listen with more pleasure to people singing songs that they happen to know already than to songs that they do not know? Is it because *it is more obvious when the singer hits his target* (in Greek *skopos), as it were, if they know the piece being sung*?

Ps.-Aristotle, *Problems* 19.5, transl. Mayhew 2011, italics mine

When people listen to imitations, *their feelings are always changed in sympathy with them (pantes sympatheis)*, even when there are no words (*chōris logōn*, with Susehmil's emendation), *owing to the rhythms and melodies themselves.*

Aristotle, *Politics* 8.1340a12f., transl. Barker 1984 with slight modifications, italics mine

In the two quotations from the Peripatetic *Problems* (a text gradually assembled by the Peripatetic school from the third century BCE, written in a question-and-answer format), the emotional synchrony between the performer and the listener is fostered by a shared experience, i.e. the familiarity with the same melody, which prompts the two of them to sing together – a phenomenon that is familiar to all of us who, as teenagers, attended a concert put on by our favourite singer. This observation is confirmed by another passage in the same book, *Problems* 19.9. Here we are told that, when someone sings to the accompaniment of a single aulos or lyre instead of many (which would obscure the song), the melody is more enjoyable because the listener perceives more clearly the moment in which the singer hits the target (*skopos*), i.e. when the melody has developed as the listener expects (Raffa 2017, 16f.: all these passages seem to imply that cognition is involved, cf. Huron 2008). The occurrence in the *Politics*, however, adds a rather intriguing remark. According to it, human beings tend not only to resonate with the emotional atmosphere that emanates from other people. The same psychological mechanism is at work – Aristotle suggests – when the emotion, expressed by music thanks to its mimetic capacity (III.3), activates a similar motor representation in the observer/perceiver.[24] To put it simply, the listener is moved to feel the same emotion that music represents, as is argued by modern *arousal theory* which explains the expressiveness of music as its propensity to evoke the corresponding emotion in the listener (Davies 2010). This happens, Aristotle seems to be saying, without the listener being aware of the causal mechanisms responsible for this transmission. In the same way an audience, while watching a tragedy, is induced to feel the same *pathē*, i.e. pity and fear, felt by the characters in the drama to the point of being purified by it (see Aristotle *Poetics* 6.11449b, quoted at I.4, esp. n. 58).[25] The way Aristotle develops this idea in the following lines of the *Politics* (1340a18–25) suggests that this process of emotional contagion occurs without any explicit cognitive mediation; the emotional reactions to musical likenesses (*homoiōmata*), he says, are similar to the reactions we have to the realities themselves (*pros tēn alētheian*, lit. 'towards actual reality', cf. 1340a23–5). This effect is peculiar to musical *mimēmata* (i.e. 'imitations'). In other objects of perception, such as those of touch and taste, there are no likenesses of moral characteristics or emotional patterns, but rather 'signs' (*sēmeia*) of them. This sometimes happens with the objects of sight, which at the most serve as a mark (*episēma*) to distinguish emotions (1340a23–35); the mark stimulates a cognitive passage, through which we become able to identify the emotion to which a painting, for instance, refers (on *episēma* as an aid to memory, see Aristotle *On Memory* 1.450b20f.). That's why rhythms and melodies have a special status among the other objects of perception. They are able both to contain – not only 'be signs of' – and to arouse *pathē* in the listeners, without the need for any mediation, cf. 1340a18–20: 'there exist in rhythms and melodies likenesses of anger and mildness' (transl. Barker 1984).

Aristotle's observations challenge us to want to know more about the putative cause of this expressive capacity of *mousikē*. A partial answer to the question may be found in other two passages of the pseudo-Aristotelian *Problems*, which appear to be closely connected with the part of the *Politics* we have been discussing so far:

Why is it that what is heard (*to akouston*), alone among perceptibles, has *ēthos*? For even if there is a melody (*melos*) without words (*logos*), it has *ēthos* none the less, but neither colour nor smell nor flavour have it. Is it because it alone has movement (*kinēsis*), though not the movement that the sound stirs up in us, since that kind of movement exists in the other perceptibles too (thus colour moves the vision)? But we perceive the movement that follows upon a sound of this kind (i.e., a sound that is part of a melodic sequence). This movement has likeness (*homoiotēs*) both in rhythms and in the ordering of high and low notes, though not in their mixture: a concord (*symphōnia*) has no *ēthos*. This *ēthos* does not exist in any other perceptibles. But the movements themselves are related to action (*praktikai*), and actions are indications (*sēmasia*) of character.

Ps.-Aristotle, Problems 19.27, transl. Barker 1984,
slightly modified

Why do rhythms and melodies, which are sound (*phōnē*), resemble ethical characters, while flavours do not, nor colours and odours? Is it because they are movements (*kinēseis*), as actions (*praxeis*) also are? Now activity (*energeia*) is ethical and produces ethical character, but flavours and colours do not act in this way.

Ps.-Aristotle, Problems 19.29, transl. Mayhew 2011

The movement we perceive when we listen to music – a movement which has in itself, the author says, a likeness to *ēthos*, which we may here interpret as the *aesthetic* character of a specific piece of music – is not the same movement that is generally produced by any sensory stimulus, as happens when we perceive objects of any other sense. It is a movement following (*hepomenē*) melodic or rhythmic elements which are part of a melodic sequence or a rhythmic pattern, as if to say, it has to do with *dynamic*, not static elements, since *music moves through time*. What happens when we hear a rhythmically articulate melody is very different, the author clarifies, from the reaction we may have when hearing a *symphōnia*, that is, a musical concord (like the octave, the most perfect among the consonances for the Greeks, see II.2),[26] since we perceive *symphōnia* as a motionless mixture of sounds, not as a sequence of events flowing along through time.[27] This is the reason why melodies and rhythms have similarities with human actions and activities – because both are *energeia*, i.e. 'activity'. This means that the most significant resemblance to the human expression of emotions relies in music's dynamic and processional character.

There is no doubt that melodic and rhythmic motions play an important role in emotional reactions to music; human beings tend to synchronize their internal rhythm to the periodicities that are present in the temporal structure of the music. Modern cognitive neuroscience has been studying our reactions to music's temporal structure for a long time, with the result that nowadays we know which regions of the brain are involved in tracking the temporal flow of sound sequences and thus we can better understand which sympathetic and parasympathetic pathways drive our psychophysiological reactions to music (like respiration, cardiac activity and blood pressure: Levitin 2009; Trost and Vuilleumier 2013). We have evidence for an interest towards these issues in antiquity too, as in the theoretical treatise *On Music* written by Aristides Quintilianus (third–fourth century CE). Book 2 of this work, whose goal is 'to show how excellent a branch of learning music is' (*On Music* 1.2, transl. Barker 1989), focuses on the value of music in education and in psychiatric therapy. In chapter 15, the author discusses rhythms and their corresponding emotional effects on human beings; rhythms that give an initial calm to the mind by beginning from the down-beat (as the dactylic rhythm: — U U) are more peaceful, while those that transmit the beat to the voice by beginning from the up-beat (e.g. the iambic rhythm: U —) are restless; rhythms composed of short syllables (hence running quickly) are most swift and passionate, while those composed only of long syllables are slower and calm and so on (*On Music* 2.15).[28] While describing the effects of long durations of time in sacred hymns, the concern is on the physiological effect on the listeners. The discourse returns to these aspects also when the focus is on compound rhythms, i.e. rhythms generated by the mixture of different genera:

> In using these extended durations people displayed their concern for things sacred, and their attachment to them, and by the equality and length of the durations they also brought their minds into a state of good order, believing that this was what constituted the health of the soul. *That is why, in the movements of the pulse too, the healthiest people are those in whom contraction and dilation answer to one another through movements of these kinds.* [...] Compound

rhythms are more emotional (*pathētikōteroi*), because for the most part the rhythms from which they are constituted are unequal [...] Those that remain within a single genus are less disturbing, while those that modulate to others pull the soul violently in opposite directions, forcing it through their multiplicity to follow and assimilate itself to every variation. Thus, it is also true that *those movements of the arteries which keep the same form, though varying slightly in their durations, are disordered but not dangerous, while those that alter too much in their durations, or go so far as to change from one genus to another, are frightening and deadly.*

Aristides Quintilianus, On Music 2.15,
transl. Barker 1989, italics mine

In this passage, Aristides Quintilianus relies on the authority of earlier medical scientists such as Herophilus (*c.* 335–250 BCE), who had developed the theory of the diagnostic value of the pulse and studied it in connection with the rhythmic ratios in music, according to what we are later told by Galen (*c.* 129–201 CE): 'as the musicians establish their rhythms according to certain definite arrangements of time-periods, comparing the arsis and thesis with one another [that is, the upward and the downward beat], so Herophilus supposes that the dilatation of the artery corresponds to arsis and its contraction to thesis' (Galen, *Synopsis of His Sixteenth Books on the Pulse* 9.464, transl. Lloyd 1973; cf. van Staden 1989, 276–88). This confirms what I have said at the beginning of the paragraph: ancient Greek speculation on the emotional induction operated by music put great emphasis on the *embodiment* of emotions. The theme was repeatedly taken up in the following centuries, e.g. by Marsilio Ficino (II.3), who in his commentary on Plato's *Timaeus*, while exploring the physiological basis for music therapy and the induction of emotions, agrees with the view that duration and intensity of heartbeats correspond to specific musical proportions (Prins 2012). Similar remarks have recently been made also by modern embodiment theories of the mind. They have challenged the widespread dualistic approach to the theme of emotions by suggesting that the body helps to constitute the mind in shaping emotional responses (Varela, Thompson and Rosch 1991; Barrett and Lindquist 2008; Shapiro and Spaulding 2021).

3. Mimetic paradigms

The Peripatetic sources we have quoted so far describe the capacity of music to express human emotions as depending on some intrinsically musical features, such as melodic sequences and rhythmic patterns. More often, however, the Greeks discuss the response to *mousikē* as object-directed, as if the response is ultimately made to the music's content rather than to music itself, in the belief that the capacity of music to move the soul – i.e. its psychagogic power – relies on some external elements that music imitates or represents somehow. This is why the remarks of the Greek writers so frequently focus on the evaluation and selection of its most suitable content. The mimetic conception of music and, more generally, of art was highly influential in Western aesthetics at least until the mid-eighteenth century, when it began to be contested and then completely rejected by Romantic expressivism. But Greek *mimēsis* was a more complex concept than it would later become and it cannot be interpreted as mere copying or duplication. The history and interpretation of this idea and a better assessment of its legacy have undergone a major revision in recent scholarship. Thanks to scholars like Stephen Halliwell (2002), in fact, nowadays we interpret *mimēsis* as a family of concepts (with many uses outside philosophy), which range from simple mimetic mirroring to enactive mimesis, i.e. indicating all the imagined possibilities of experience suggested by artistic representations, being fully aware that no single modern equivalent can appropriately translate this word in all its wide range of meanings (Woodruff 2015).

The mimetic character of *mousikē* is discussed by many authors of Greek antiquity, the most influential of which are certainly Plato and Aristotle. What has always made it difficult to talk about imitation in musical art is to understand *how* music can represent content by means of pure sounds and *what* precisely its contents are, questions that Greek philosophers tried to answer in their time. In the famous opening of his *Poetics* (1447a13 ff.), where he gives a detailed list of all the artistic and competitive practices conceived as *mimēseis* (epic poetry, tragedy and comedy, dithyrambic poetry, as well as instrumental musical genres), Aristotle explains that all these *technai* produce a representation using rhythm, speech and melody, either separately or mixed, and the objects of their representation are characters (*ēthē*), emotions (*pathē*) and actions (*praxeis*, 1447a28), i.e. the basic ingredients of human life. In Aristotle's *The Art of Rhetoric*, indeed, we find the same interweaving of elements:

> Let us now describe the nature of the *characters* of men according to their *emotions*, habits, ages, and fortunes. By the emotions I mean anger, desire, and the like, of which we have already spoken; by habits virtues and vices, of which also we have previously spoken, as well as *the kind of things men individually and deliberately choose and practice*.
>
> 　　　　　　　*The Art of Rhetoric* 2.1388b31–6, transl. Freese,
> 　　　　　　　　　　　rev. by Striker 2020, italics mine

Clearly Aristotle, and many other Greeks with him, believed that any kind of mimetic art, even purely instrumental music (cf. Plato, *Laws* 2.669e1–670a3), could convey and express specific meanings and complex narratives and that the means by which *mousikē* realizes its mimetic content are its most technical components.[29] To confirm this, while discussing the nature of sound and auditory perception, Aristotle states that *phōnē* is a sound that means something (*sēmantikos*) and that it always appears *meta phantasias*, i.e. it is accompanied by a sensorial and mental after-image activated by music's representational power (*On the Soul* 420b31–4).[30] Such a mimetic idea of *mousikē* was certainly widespread in ancient Greece, although not ubiquitous. Some philosophers, like Aristoxenus, do not mention it at all when discussing music's expressiveness while others, such as the Epicurean Philodemus, deny that music could convey extra-musical contents (III.1). The latter can be considered a forerunner of modern formalists who believe that absolute, i.e. instrumental, music has neither representational nor semantic content, its meaning being determined only by its *formal* structure, as affirmed by Eduard Hanslick (1825–1904), the music critic commonly regarded as the founder of musical formalism in aesthetics. In his treatise *The Beautiful in Music* (Leipzig 1854), Hanslick says that music 'not only speaks by means of sound, it speaks nothing but sound' (Hanslick 1891 [1854], 163). More recent developments of this theory, as the aesthetic approach elaborated by the musicologist Peter Kivy (who talks about *enhanced formalism*), take into account not only the formal structure of sounds but also their syntactic features, consisting of melodic and rhythmic passages – such as repetition, contrast, resolution and so on – that happen *in* the music (Kivy 2002, 88–109).

In spite of these isolated dissenting voices, the persistence of the belief in the mimetic character of music lasted for a long time, up to Late Antiquity. An interesting discussion on musical mimesis is included in the already mentioned treatise *On Music* by Aristides Quintilianus (third–fourth century CE). In this work, well-known Platonic and Peripatetic notions are supplemented with Neoplatonic and Stoic ideas. In Book 2, ch. 4, the author declares his intention to give a reply 'to those who doubt whether everyone is moved by melody' (55.24–6, transl. Barker 1989), clearly echoing Aristotelian concerns expressed in Book 8 of the *Politics* (cf. I.3); but he also admits that different people are affected in different ways by the same kind of music (55.30–56.5), a topic discussed at length throughout the whole book.[31] Aristides starts his explanation by pointing out how human learning comes from similarities (*di'homoiotētōn*), 'which we assess by bringing them to the attention of our senses (*tais aisthēsesin epiballontes*)' (56.6f.). *Mousikē*, he says, is much more efficient than any other kind of art in moving the soul, for it realizes its imitation through several senses, being a blending of poetry (*poiēsis*), melody (*melōidia*) and rhythms (*rhythmoi*). Pure poetry, with the medium of words alone, is not always capable of arousing emotions but, with melody, it becomes able to set them in motion (*kinei*) while, thanks to rhythms, it can bring the emotions 'into conformity with its subject matter (*oikeioi tois hypokeimenois*)' (56.10–14). In fact, only music 'teaches both by words (*kai logōi*) and by images of actions (*kai praxeōn eikosi*), and through agents that are not static or fixed in a single pattern but are alive (*di'empsychōn*), and alter their form and their movement to fit every detail of what the words express' (56.17–21). Here the focus, as in some passages of Aristotle's *Politics* and *Poetics*, is on the great capacity of the technical elements of music to perfectly adhere and give value to its (verbal) *contents*, which correspond to behaviours and actions performed by human beings. In fact, while the other imitative arts are not able to bring us quickly to a conception (*ennoia*) of the action they represent, *mousikē* 'persuades more directly and effectively (*energestata*), since the means by which it makes its imitation are of just the same kind as those by which the actions themselves are accomplished in reality' (56.27–57.2). Then follows an interesting explanation of the similarities between human behaviour and its mimesis through music. As, in actual events, deliberation comes first, speech follows and last comes the performance of an action, in the same way these three elements of the process are imitated by music: 'music imitates the characters and emotions of the soul through its conceptions (*ennoiai*), speech through *harmoniai* and the moulding of the voice, action through rhythm and bodily movement' (57.2–6). In this and other passages of the treatise, the moral or emotional content that the artist seeks to convey through music is indicated by the technical term *ennoia*. It is a Stoic notion that performs an active role in the process of concept-formation, since it refers to the way in which the soul represents something to itself in thought (Dyson 2009). As Aristides also makes clear in later chapters, *ennoia* has a leading role among the elements of which *mousikē* is composed: 'The four main objectives at which the musical educator should aim are these: suitability of idea (*ennoia*), of diction, of *harmonia*, and of rhythm. The idea is in all respects the leader, since without it there can be no choice or rejection of anything' (2.7, 65.22–6). Clearly, it is the *content* – here openly described in the conceptual representation that the soul makes of it to itself[32] – that necessarily drives all the other components of music, as we had been told by Plato in *Republic* 3.398d: *harmonia* and rhythm must *follow* the words. However, Aristides adds, since each human being has a different nature and, consequently, his/her emotions are differently disposed, differences of conception (*ennoia*) may also arise. This is why each individual takes pleasure in different kinds of music (2.8, 67.15–68.13 and *passim*).

4. Musical beauty

The relativism and (partial) subjectivity that Aristides seems to introduce in his discussion on musical *mimesis*, even without mentioning *taste* (which will become fundamental only in modern philosophical discussions on art, as in the famous essay *On the Standard of Taste* of the philosopher David Hume, 1711–76, published in 1757), are atypical for ancient Greek philosophers. Usually they rather tend to a sort of aesthetic universalism and objectivity in identifying the qualities to be appreciated in music.[33] Especially in authors who firmly believed in the mimetic conception of *mousikē*, the *beauty* of music ultimately coincides with the *goodness* of the imitated models, i.e. the virtues represented the musical works, clearly identifying aesthetic with ethical goodness, as in Plato, *Laws* 2.655a: since 'all the postures (*schēmata*) and melodies (*melē*) belonging to goodness of soul or body, to virtue itself or any image of it, are good (*kala*)' (transl. Barker 1984; Halliwell 2002, 65, calls this approach 'ethical aesthetics'). The elements that are meant to convey what is beautiful (*to kalon*) in music are the formal structures on which dances and melodies are built, namely dance figures, scales and patterns of attunement; their excellence relies on the harmonious convergence of elements that realize a correct correspondence to the mimetic model and present themselves to our perception in a pleasant way.

But what are these distinguishing features that, for the Greeks, make music *beautiful*? Authors embracing the mathematical approach to harmonic theory were inclined to connect aesthetic excellence in the acoustic domain to harmonic or symmetrical relationships between sounds, as in the case of concords (*symphōniai*, cf. II.2). *Symphōniai* were paradigmatic examples of the harmonious integration and blending of two elements expressed in mathematically beautiful ratios. See, e.g., Aristotle, *On Sense and Sensible Objects* 439b31–3, where the *goodness* (here not further clarified) of the ratios between the components of a mixture is openly described as the cause of its pleasantness: 'For on this view the colours that depend on *numbers with good ratios* (*eulogistoi arithmoi*), like the concords in music, are regarded as the most attractive (*hēdista*)' (transl. Hett 1957, slightly adapted).[34] More interestingly, in an Aristotelian fragment of uncertain origin, the marvellous symmetry of musical *harmonia* – i.e. the octave scale conceived as an articulated system with a specific internal structure, cf. I.4 – is praised as celestial (*ourania*) and its nature is said to be divine (*theia*), beautiful (*kalē*) and wonderful (*daimonia*) just in virtue of its mathematical framework. The arithmetic and harmonic means divide the octave-scale in structures (tetrachords) and intervals (fourths and fifths), making it worthy of aesthetic admiration:[35]

Harmonia is celestial, and its nature is divine, beautiful and wonderful. In potential it is four-fold, and it has two means, the arithmetic and the harmonic; and its parts, magnitudes and excesses are revealed in accordance with number and equal measure; for melodies acquire their structure in two tetrachords.[36]

Aristotle fr. 47 Rose, transl. Barker 2007

Interestingly, appreciation of similar qualities was also expressed by those authors who did not advocate a mathematical interpretation of audible sounds, like Aristoxenus. Indeed, the structural patterns on which the melodies are built remain equally significant for him; what he praises more in music is the 'remarkable orderliness' (*thaumastē taxis*) of the arrangement of melodic – as well as rhythmic – elements in composition (*Elements of Harmonics* 5.23–9, cf. *Elements of Rhythmics* 4.19–22). He believes that the principles governing the synthesis of every interval with every other are essential for obtaining what he calls 'the attuned melody' (*to hērmosmenon melos*), i.e. the only musical melody which is worthy of the name. Its correctness and beauty are determined not by the musician's creativity but by the nature (*physis*) of melody itself, that has an innate tendency to move or change in specific ways (*Elements of Harmonics* 18.5–19.11).[37] The connection between beauty and proportion is made more explicit in an Aristoxenian fragment belonging to a work titled *Pythagorean Precepts*, whose contents describe the rules of behaviour of fourth-century BCE Pythagoreans. In fr. 35 Wehrli, while talking about the Pythagorean precepts in matters of education, Aristoxenus reports that, according to them, the *paideia* of the youth should follow the principle that order (*taxis*) and due proportion (*symmetria*) are beautiful (*kala*) and advantageous, while disorder and lack of due proportion are ugly and disadvantageous. He does not explicitly endorse the Pythagorean opinion here, but a similar way of describing education may be read in his fr. 76 Wehrli, which comes from a biographical work devoted to Telesias, a Theban composer and performer of the fourth century BCE (for a comment on this passage, see Barker 2007, 247–9). Here Aristoxenus describes the beauty of ancient music (*kallistē mousikē*) as relying on specific melodic and rhythmic elements, whose learning and experience since childhood provided Telesias with an excellent training (*kallistē agōgē*) and made it impossible for him to practise the complicated new style of music of some late fifth/early fourth-century composers: Philoxenus of Cythera (*c*. 435–380 BCE) and Timotheus of Miletus (*c*. 450–360 BCE).

Overall, philosophers concerned both with mathematical and empirical harmonics link beauty to similar concepts – proportion and symmetry on the one hand, order and arrangement on the other, notions all related to the fittingness of the components of musical structures into a coherent whole (see the notion of *harmonia* discussed at I.4) – and claim universal validity for their recognition (for the centrality of similar concepts in modern aesthetics, see Scruton 2009, 126). Appeals to these notions are quite usual in Greek discussions of beauty. Aristotle, in the *Poetics*, compares well-constructed plots with beautiful animals or objects (7.1450b37: 'beauty consists in magnitude and order', transl. Halliwell 1995) while, in the *Metaphysics*, he more explicitly relates the notion of beauty to quantitative mathematical principles (13.3.1078a36–1078b2: 'The main species of beauty are orderly arrangement, proportion, and definiteness; and these are especially manifested by the mathematical sciences', transl. Tredennick 1935). *Eurhythmia*, lit. 'good proportion', and *symmetria*, i.e. 'symmetry', are undoubtedly key terms of the Greek aesthetic vocabulary. They were developed in the fields of both music theory and the visual arts since at least the classical period (e.g. *The Canon* of the sculptor Polyclitus) and still used in Roman times.[38] An example is Vitruvius' claim at the beginning of his treatise *On Architecture*, written around 15 BCE (Michon 2018). While describing the aesthetic foundations of his work, Vitruvius (*c*. 80/70–15 BCE) lists six concepts of which architecture consists. In order to do this, he borrows from other technical fields (including music) the classification tools that could provide support to his theorization: 'Architecture consists of ordering (*ordinatio*), which is called *taxis* in Greek, and of design (*dispositio*) – the Greeks call this *diathesis* – and shapeliness (*eurythmia*) and symmetry (*symmetria*) and correctness (*decor*) and allocation (*distributio*), which is called *oikonomia* in Greek' (*On Architecture* 1.2.1, transl. Rowland 1999). This need to identify attributes that are universally recognized as beautiful makes the goals of ancient Greek thought on art somewhat different from those of most modern aesthetic trends. The so-called cultural constructionism, for instance, has long since introduced a relativism of aesthetic qualities by giving value to cultural contextualization, with its specific norms and conventions, in any type of evaluation process (van Damme 1996). More recently, however, the growing fields of evolutionary psychology and empirical aesthetics have revived the search for cross-cultural features in the appreciation of art, albeit on a more biological basis (see, e.g., Dutton 2003; Sun and Che 2019; Zaidel 2019).

The Greek music theorist who, more than others, sought to demonstrate the complete agreement between a mathematical understanding of musical beauty and the evidence of sense perception is Claudius Ptolemy (*c.* 100–70 CE). From the beginning of his *Harmonics*, he discussed concords and musical beauty quite extensively (on the topic, see especially Barker 2010). In Book 1 chapter 5 (titled 'Concerning the principles adopted by the Pythagoreans in their postulates about the concords'),[39] he says that the ratios underlying concords – i.e., multiple and epimoric ratios – are finer (*kallion*, lit. 'more beautiful') because of the 'simplicity of the comparison' (*haplotēs tēs parabolēs*). This means that, if the two terms of a ratio share a measure – as in a multiple ratio, for instance, where the smaller term is a unit by which the larger can be measured –, the process of comparison between them is easier to grasp and makes their relationship more pleasing for perception as well. Concerns about beauty (*to kalon*) return in *Harmonics* 3.3, where the relationship between reason and hearing, investigated from the very beginning of the treatise (*Harmonics* 1.1), is further explored. Here, besides describing the role of reason in discovering order (*taxis*) and *symmetria* in audible things, Ptolemy emphasizes the capacity of sight and hearing to judge 'their objects not only by the standard of pleasure (*hēdonē*), but also, much more importantly, by that of beauty (*to kalon*)', since 'no one would classify the beautiful (*to kalon*) and the ugly (*to aischron*) as belonging to things touched or tasted or smelled, but only to things seen and things heard, such as shape and melody, or the movement of the heavenly bodies, or human actions' (transl. Barker 1989). Ptolemy is clearly confirming the equivalence between beauty and proportion among the parts, as in any other ancient Greek account on the topic (Huffmann 2010). In addition to this, however, he also gives a much clearer and broader value to the role of perception in the cognitive evaluation process of audible (and visual) phenomena, although the causes of beauty remain essentially a matter of numbers and are, thus, regarded as entirely objective.

Occurrences and Recurrences

1. *Ancient* vs *modern* quarrels

Musical styles, genres and technicalities evolve through time: later composers and performers always build on the work of their predecessors and no change comes out the blue. Some events in the history of music are certainly more groundbreaking than others (see Introduction), but the way they are interpreted depends on what they signify to their observers. The reception of artistic, intellectual and technical transformations in the field of music as a novelty, in antithesis to something older, is a matter of perception; it can be presented as such for purposes of propaganda, cultural appropriation or, rather, as a way of differentiating from the past (on the theme of 'the new' in classical Greece, see especially D'Angour 2011: on music, see ch. 8, 184–206). As structural sociology and anthropology have demonstrated, elements of human culture are better understood in relation to one another, i.e. as binary oppositions. This is why the formation and shaping of musical or, more broadly, cultural trends in terms of contrasting dualities are found in many eras and different cultures.[1]

Quarrels between *ancients* and *moderns* – the same pairing of terms that gives the title to the series to which this book belongs – have characterized many historical periods of Western culture, such as the famous *Querelle des Anciens et des Modernes* that inflamed the literary and artistic debate in late seventeenth-century France, with significant antecedents in Italy (Fumaroli 2001). This is especially true in the field of music. To cite a few examples, the sophisticated forms of sacred and secular polyphony created in France and Italy during the fourteenth and early fifteenth centuries are conventionally labelled *Ars Nova* (lit. 'New Art'), as opposed to the thirteenth-century *Ars Antiqua* (lit. 'Ancient Art').[2] Between the Renaissance and the Baroque, the dichotomy between ancient and modern music remained a central issue for many decades, shifting its focus according to the people involved: the famous controversy between Vincenzo Galilei and his former teacher Zarlino about the systems of intonation used at the time (II.2) found its manifesto in Galilei's *Dialogue of Ancient and Modern Music* (Florence 1581), while in the early years of the seventeenth century the debate between *musica antica* and *moderna* ('ancient' and 'modern music') was extended to two contrasting approaches to composition, especially as far as the relationship between text and music is concerned[3] (see especially Girolamo Mei's *Discourse on Ancient Music, and Modern*, Venice 1602, and Marco Scacchi's *Short Discourse about Modern Music*, Warsaw 1649).[4] Shortly afterwards, the label *stile antico* ('old style') started to be applied to sacred musical compositions that contained old-fashioned features reminiscent of Renaissance polyphony (Miller 2001). In the nineteenth century, the goal of reclaiming or reinventing aspects of *ancient* Greek culture by the European (especially German) imagination did not obscure, in the composers of the time, the awareness of their own *modern* identity (Geary 2014). With the rise of *modernism* in twentieth-century music and art (which, in turn, was then dialectically opposed by *postmodernism*), the desire to get beyond – in many ways – the musical technicalities of the past became a core value in aesthetics (Botstein 2001; Pasler 2001).[5]

It is plainly evident that the *ancient/modern* polarity has always had a major importance in Western musical culture, with Greek antiquity often cited as a source of inspiration for one of the two opposing sides (as in some of the examples quoted above). The way of presenting musical styles of different periods as opposites is frequent in ancient Greek sources too and it becomes more systematic when the historicist – i.e. teleologically oriented – analysis of literary disciplines, including *mousikē*, is successfully introduced by Aristotle and the early Peripatos.[6] Since the fifth century BCE, indeed, and more extensively in the fourth, we find plenty of passages in Greek literature in which two different styles of music – one traditional, the other modern and presented as *innovative* – are compared. It happens, for instance, when a poet advertises his own originality with respect to tradition ('I don't sing the *old* song / for my *new* songs are superior', says the late-fifth-century BCE poet Timotheus of Miletus, cf. Csapo and Wilson 2009) or in contexts where broader discussions about generational oppositions in matters of culture and education are held, as in Old Comedy.[7] In a fragment reported by two Byzantine lexicographers (Photius *b* 88 and Suda *b* 173, probably relying on a common source), the comic playwright Eupolis (*c.* 446–411 BCE) compares two distinct musical styles labelling them as *old* vs *modern*, although the lack of context does not make it clear which of the two, if either, the character actually prefers:

(A.) Come on! Do you want hear about the modern (*nun*, lit. 'now')[8] disposition of song or the old (*archaion*) style?

(B.) You'll describe both, and after I hear about them, I'll consider which of the two styles appeals to me and I'll choose.

Eupolis, fr. 326 KA, transl. Olson 2014

A similar binary opposition may be found in Aristophanes' plays (*c.* 450–386 BCE), usually in contexts that display a harsh judgmental attitude towards contemporary cultural practices. In the *Wasps* (422 BCE), for instance, the songs of one of the earliest tragedians, Phrynichus (*c.* 535–476 BCE), described as 'sweet old Sidon Songs by Phynichus' (219f. *melē archaiomelisidōnophrynichērata*, transl. Henderson 1998b),[9] are presented as the favoured repertoire by the main character of the play, the old Philocleon who, in contrast with his son Bdelycleon, constantly expresses a nostalgic longing for the good old days of the Athenian past. In the *Clouds* (423 BCE), we are told that 'old education' (*hē archaia paideusis*) taught students to memorize a song and 'to tune their voices to the mode their fathers (*hoi pateres*) handed down', in sharp contrast with 'the sort of riff today's singers (*hoi nun*) put in' (966–71, transl. Henderson 1998b). These words are said during the contest between the Better and the Worse Argument, two characters representing traditional customs, on the one side, and modern rhetorical techniques of persuasion – thought of as morally deplorable – on the other. In these and other pieces of evidence, the dispute over music is inserted within a broader social examination and assessed from a traditionalist perspective: see, e.g., *Birds* 1383–90 and *Peace* 827–31, where dithyrambic poets are harshly criticized for their poetic inconsistency, or *Women at the Thesmophoria* 25ff., mocking the tragic poet Agathon as effeminate. As a consequence, negative connotations are always attached to contemporary music, which is closely linked to moral corruption (similar to what happened in the 1950s with Rock and Roll music, considered as corrupting when it first appeared).

Greek evidence insists that, between the fifth and fourth centuries BCE, some important changes in musical language and style occurred, especially in Athens where theatrical performances were prominent. This happened especially because of the new organological possibilities of the aulos allowing for modulation between different scales. The introduction of some modulating mechanisms (rotating sleeves or, alternatively, longitudinally moving sliders covering different combinations of holes in the tube of the pipe: cf. Hagel and Terzēs 2022) is ascribed to the piper Pronomos of Thebes (late fifth century BCE), who is frequently quoted by the sources as a panhellenic star (Wilson 2007). His fame was such that he is represented as the central figure on a famous red-figure volute krater that scholars have named after him, the so-called *Pronomos Vase*, discovered in a tomb at Ruvo di Puglia, Italy, in

1835 (Taplin and Wyles 2020). The technical possibilities offered by this and other 'panharmonic' instruments (lit. on which it is possible to play 'all the *harmoniai*', see Plato, *Republic* 3.399c–d) affected many contexts and poetic genres in antiquity – especially dithyramb, kitharodic solos and drama – contributing to the rise of virtuosos (instrumental players and singers) and leading to a wide-ranging cultural phenomenon that modern scholars have labelled as New Music (see, e.g., Csapo 2004; D'Angour 2020). The most important evidence for the scorn poured on this phenomenon by ancient conservatives is a famous fragment (fr. 155 KA) from the comedy *Cheiron* of the poet Pherecrates (late fifth century BCE). Here Lady Music, i.e. the personification of *mousikē* represented on stage in the guise of a woman, complains about the violence she has suffered at the hands of the musicians of her time (see, e.g., Restani 1983; Gianvittorio 2018). This fragment is quoted in a dialogue titled *On Music* (30.1141d–1142a), a compilation handed down under the name of Plutarch (whose author, however, is actually unknown) which, although written between the first and the second century CE (that is, in the time of Plutarch), is largely based on fourth-century BCE material, mainly Peripatetic (i.e. Aristoxenus of Tarentum (*c*. 370/65–? BCE) and Heraclides of Pontus (*c*. 387–312 BCE)).[10] The entire narrative of the fictitional symposium in which the dialogue is set (the host of the feast is the rich Onesicrates, who addresses questions to two experts on the topic of music, Lysias and Soterichus) is realized as a sharp polarization between the past and the present, i.e. the *archaia mousikē* practised by the elders (*hoi palaioi*) and the modern style of music of the contemporaries (*hoi nun*, understood from the chronological perspective of the fourth-century sources of the dialogue), constantly 'comparing the older compositions (*ta tote*) with those of today (*ta nun*)' (*On Music* 21.1138b, transl. Barker 1984).[11] Such a contrast, already present in a large number of sources of the classical period, becomes the framework of the entire dialogue, supporting the development of a historical model strongly influenced by fourth-century BCE Peripatetic sources in which aetiology, i.e. the desire to identify the origin of a cultural phenomenon, intertwines with a teleological view (Tocco 2019). That is to say, discoveries and innovations in art and literature do not follow one another by accident, but rather converge towards a specific end (on teleology in history, see Carr 2020).

The peculiarity of this dialogue would determine its fortune in later times. It would be one of the earliest Greek works on music translated into Latin in the Renaissance (its translation by the humanist scholar Carlo Valgulio (*c.* 1434–1517) was published in Brescia in 1507 and reprinted several times until 1572), becoming one of the most read texts by the humanists of the time (Meriani 2022). In the preface to the dialogue (*Proemium in Musicam Plutarchi*, see Meriani 2015 and 2019), written in the form of a letter-treatise, Valgulio draws an explicit parallel between the criticism displayed in the Plutarchan work and the decadence of the music of his own time. In the sixteenth century, indeed, pseudo-Plutarch's *On Music* easily became an authoritative model for scholarly discussions on the intricacies of contemporary music by suggesting an analogous return to the (supposed) simplicity of ancient *mousikē*.

A decisive impulse to this contrast of values embedded in the ancient vs modern dichotomy, however, had been provided much earlier. In Book 3 of the *Laws*, Plato (*c.* 428/427–348/347 BCE) offers his famous (and influential) nostalgic description of the music of the past (*hē tote mousikē*, whose types and forms, he says, were properly distinguished as it was not permitted to use one type of melody for the purpose of another), contrasting it sharply with the degeneration of fourth-century law-breaking compositions:

> **Ath.**   Under the ancient laws, my friends, our common people were not masters of anything, but were in a sort of way voluntary slaves to the laws.
>
> **Meg.**   What laws do you mean?

Ath. Those, first of all, to do *with the music they had then* (*peri tēn mousikēn* [. . .] *tēn tote*), if we are to describe the growth of the excessively liberated life from its beginning. In those days our music was divided into various types and forms. One type of song consisted of prayers to the gods, the name given to these being 'hymns'. There was another type, the opposite of the first, which one might best call 'lamentations': another consisted of paeans, and there was another, invented, I think by Dionysus, known as the 'dithyramb'. To another class of song they assigned the name '*nomoi*' itself, adding the title 'kitharodic'. With these types and various others properly distinguished, it was not permitted to use one type of melody for the purposes of another. [. . .] But *later, as time went on*, there appeared as instigators of *unmusical law-breaking composers* who, though by nature skilled at composition, were *ignorant of what is right and lawful in music*. In a Bacchic frenzy, and enthralled beyond what is right by pleasure, they mixed lamentations with hymns and paeans with dithyrambs, imitated aulos songs with their kithara songs, and put everything together with everything else, thus unintentionally, through their stupidity, giving false witness against music, alleging that music possesses no standard of correctness, but is most correctly judged by the pleasure of the person who enjoys it, whether he is a better man or a worse. By creating compositions of these kinds and by choosing corresponding words, they inspired the masses with lawlessness towards music, and the effrontery to suppose that they were capable of judging it. As a result the audiences, which had been silent, became noisy, as if they understood what is good in music and what is not, and *a musical aristocracy was displaced by a degenerate theatrocracy*. Now no doubt it would have been no very terrible thing if a democracy of free men had arisen just in the field of music: but in fact, from a starting-point in music, everyone came to believe in their own wisdom about everything, and to reject the law, and liberty followed immediately [. . .].

Plato, *Laws* 3.700a–701b, transl. Barker 1984, italics mine

The polarization between *ancient* and *modern* music is here emphasized by including terms and concepts related to the semantic field of *law*, with the aim of describing modern deviations from a more traditional repertoire (Rocconi 2016a).[12] The double meaning of the term *nomos* ('idiom, custom', but also 'law') makes it possible for Plato to identify in the *kitharōidikoi nomoi* – solo pieces performed by professional singers accompanying themselves with the kithara (Figure 8) – the same purity and strictness which he regards as crucial in the proper education of citizens and to ascribe these same features to any music performed in such an imaginary golden age. Actually, this etymological connection between special categories of musical composition and the inviolability of their regulations finds no support in pre-Platonic evidence. It should, rather, be interpreted within Plato's wider reasoning on artistic mimesis (III.3); he believes that all the elements of a musical composition need to be consistent with one another in order to convey the most appropriate ethical values and instil them in the citizens (see especially *Laws* 7.802d–e). Precisely by virtue of the widespread criticism against the representatives of the New Music I described above, however, these remarks have been taken literally by later sources and misinterpreted as a historical account of ancient musical practices. This has led to a distorted image of old-time *mousikē* in post-Platonic evidence such as the one we find in the pseudo-Plutarchan dialogue, where we read the famous definition – echoed for centuries – of *nomos* as a musical genre that has to conform to its own fixed patterns *by law*:

> In the old days kithara songs were not allowed to be performed as they are now, or to include modulations of *harmoniai* and rhythms, since in each *nomos the pitch which belonged to it* was maintained throughout. This is why these pieces were given their name: they were called '*nomoi*' because *deviation from the form of pitching established for each type was not permitted.*
>
> Ps.-Plutarch, On Music 6.1133b-c,
transl. Barker 1984, italics mine

Figure 8 Professional performer of a kitharodic *nomos*. Athenian red-figure amphora (*c*. 490 BCE): New York (USA), Metropolitan Museum 56.171.38.

The source of this part of the dialogue is Heraclides of Pontus, pupil of Plato who also studied with Aristotle, author of a 'Collection of [unspecified items] in music' (*Synagōgē tōn en mousikēi*) that clearly summarizes in a simplistic way some of the themes addressed by Plato in a much more complex picture.[13] Lacking the conceptual framework behind Plato's observations (i.e. the mimetic nature of musical art and the necessary convergence of its various components towards a unique and virtuous mimetic model), this presumed golden age of *mousikē* has continued to be interpreted as a historical account of real phenomena (see, e.g., Suda *n* 478, where we are told that each *nomos* has a specific attunement and rhythm), fuelling the quarrel between *ancient* and *modern* music over the centuries to come (with a growing interweaving of music and politics, see IV.3).

2. The classics and the popular

The type of polarization described above is only one of the contrasting dualities that have led to the perceived distinctiveness of a category of music from some others, inducing the people of different eras to canonize a musical repertoire to the detriment of others. Lists of authors worthy of selection were already made in classical antiquity, as the so-called Lyric Canon of the nine most representative Greek *melopoioi* (i.e. 'composers of songs/*melē*'), attested since the second century BCE but certainly shaped much earlier (Hadjimichael 2019; Nagy 2020).[14] The sharp distinction between *classical* and *popular* music that we experience nowadays, however, not only in terms of different repertoires, contexts and audiences, but also (still in some cases) of opposed qualitative values,[15] was not perceived exactly as such in antiquity. It is rather the result of a long and diversified process of selection and assessment. The designation *classic* in the sense of *example of excellence* in the literary field was already current in Roman times at least from the second century CE (Aulus Gellius, *Attic Nights* 19.8.15; cf. Citroni 2006) in the context of the mutation of the socio-economic and military lexicon; *classici* were the members of the first class, in the hierarchy of Roman citizens (on the *classical* as an ideological construct, see Schein 2011; Hall 2011). Nevertheless, only in recent times, i.e. from the mid-nineteenth century, the term has been adopted to indicate a musical repertoire, the so-called *classical music* that Western culture has chosen as an emblem of excellence and canonized as the culmination of its tradition; no ancient term corresponds to the complex of qualities connoted by this modern word (D'Angour 2006; von Glahn and Broyles 2013).

It is much harder to define the term *popular* in reference to music. Its meaning has shifted historically; *popularity* has often been linked with a specific social group, e.g. the music of common people (thus idealizing it as the *vox populi*), or with specific means of dissemination, i.e. the mass media, whose development had a significant role in the mainstream distribution of music. For modern musicology, *popular music* is an umbrella term. It encompasses a great variety of musical genres which are, broadly speaking, readily accessible to large numbers of listeners. The label is conventionally conceived of as one of the three classificatory categories of music in contemporary taxonomy, together with *art* (or *classical*) and *folk music*.[16]

Scholars in Classical Studies have tentatively identified the category of the popular with a poetic and musical repertoire (collectively labelled as *carmina popularia*, lit. 'popular songs', in the standard edition of Greek lyric poets: Page 1962) that was devoid of authorship, never institutionalized nor (intentionally) transmitted in written form – in virtue of being subject to continuous reworking to be adapted to new needs and contexts – and which has reached us only indirectly, thanks to fortuitous transmission. Therefore it appears *submerged*, according to an effective definition introduced some years ago by the Italian scholar Luigi Enrico Rossi and recently reaffirmed by his former pupils.[17] No emic category actually existed in antiquity; the *pandēmos mousikē*, i.e. 'people's music', quoted by Aristoxenus of Tarentum in a passage of a lost work dedicated to sympotic questions (*Symmikta sympotika*), simply refers to the broad consensus, in terms of audience, of the new musical styles of the fourth century BCE. Nevertheless, the context in which this expression appears gives it a clearly derogatory sense: 'We are actually in the same situation for our theatres have been barbarized, and popular music (*pandēmos mousikē*, i.e. 'that everyone likes') itself has been utterly degraded, and only a few of us recall privately what music was once like' (Aristoxenus fr. 124 Wehrli, transl. Olson 2011).[18] Nowadays we are fully aware that the repertoire of ancient Greek song can hardly be captured in modern dichotomies. A growing distance between *high* culture (i.e. erudite, shared by a few people) and *low* culture (i.e. more widely disseminated) has been attested since the Hellenistic period, from the third century BCE onwards, and it was especially due to a progressive diversification of the contexts in which poetry could be experienced. On the one hand, the circle of learned and cultivated poets of the Alexandria Museum composed their own verses for sole recitation or private reading in imitation of the lyric repertoire of the past.[19] On the other hand, different forms of spectacular entertainment of a theatrical type continued to be performed throughout the Greek-speaking world, also away from the major centres; here music played an increasingly predominant role. A hierarchy between these two categories that is also aesthetic, however, seems to be implied at least two centuries earlier, as suggested by some lines of Aristophanes' comedy *The Frogs* (405 BCE).

> [. . .] this one (sc. Euripides) takes material from everywhere: whore songs, drinking songs by Meletus, Carian pipe tunes, dirges, and dances. Someone hand me my lyre! Then again, who needs a lyre for this job? Where's that female percussionist who plays potsherds? Oh Muse of Euripides, come out here;[20] you're the proper accompanist for an recital of these songs.
>
> Aristophanes, *Frogs* 1301–7, transl. Henderson 2002

Here the tragedian Euripides (485–406 BCE), represented as a character of Aristophanes' comedy together with his colleague Aeschylus (*c.* 525–456 BCE),[21] is blamed for the *popular* (in a derogatory sense) inspiration of his music, which is said to include: whore songs and dances (like those performed by the *hetairai*, girls who were paid to brighten the evenings of symposium participants with musical as well as sexual performances, cf. IV.3); instrumental tunes with an exotic flavour (Caria was a region of Asia Minor whose mention could allude not only, generically, to something barbaric, but also to the fact that the Carians were often enlisted as mercenary soldiers, hence proverbially indicating things of little or no value); funeral songs (Plato, *Laws* 7.800e, mentions the Carian Muse, i.e. music, with reference to the choirs attending funerals for money).[22] This passage also confirms that fifth-century theatrical audiences were fully aware of and able to recognize the plurality and transversality of the musical styles performed on stage and adopted by the poets as a tool to improve dramatic action: e.g. wedding songs in marriage scenes, funeral laments when the characters were mourning the dead and so forth. Examples of popular music on the theatrical stage are frequent in Old Comedy, which usually represents lower-class characters and provides interesting insights into contemporary Athenian society. In Aristophanes' *Peace* (set in 421 BCE), for instance, the Chorus of farmers and citizens from various Greek city-states, coordinated by the god Hermes, while carrying out a rescue operation to free the goddess Peace (represented as a statue tied with ropes) from her prison inside a cave, sings two songs on stage. The rhythm and language of these verses – certainly even melodies, if we had them – hint at real work songs, which we know were widely used in antiquity to exhort physical efforts (cf. *Peace* 463: 'Heave ho! Heave ho!', transl. Henderson 1998b) and coordinate the movements in collective actions, such as reaping, grape picking, rowing and so on.[23]

Allusions to popular music, however, were not restricted to comedy. Even if, by its nature (i.e. being based on myths and hence set in heroic contexts), tragedy filtered reality more severely than comedy, some scenes of Euripides' dramas confirm what we are told by Aristophanes in the passage of the *Frogs* mentioned above. In the water-carrying scene of Euripides' *Electra* (112–66), the character of Electra – who, in this version of the myth, has been forced to wed a peasant, despite her noble origins – appears as a slave woman carrying a load of water on her head and singing a solo song, whose vocabulary oscillates between colloquial forms and threnodic expressions. Electra's working-class appearance, clearly visible also from her clothing (to such an extent

Figure 9 Women at a fountain house. Attic black-figure hydria (*c.* 510–500 BCE): New York (USA), Metropolitan Museum 06.1021.77.

that her brother Orestes does not recognize her when he sees her and takes her for a slave woman), was most probably reflected also in the music performed by the character on stage. Indeed, many folk traditions all around the world include work songs sung by women drawing and carrying water from a fountain (Figure 9).[24]

In is thus clear that, in antiquity, the languages of *high* and *low* culture interpenetrate (quoting Bakhtin) one another and are inextricably fused.[25] This makes it difficult to include a musical repertoire under the label *popular*, as the distance separating modern classifications from the ancient (still blurred) taxonomies is huge. What seems evident to me, however, is the presence of a criterion of evaluation towards specific musical repertoires which often involves social aspects and moral judgments. The dichotomies between *elitist* and *popular* culture will then become recurrent throughout history, favouring an approach to musical phenomena that is still (more or less tacitly) rooted in the contemporary way of thinking.

3. Identity, ethnicity and gender

In Greek culture, musical labels were often used to create or reinforce ethnic identities, often intertwining with the polarity of gender. When discussing music, in fact, dichotomies similar to those outlined so far (i.e. implying a value judgment) arose also in relation to ethnicity and gender. Regarding the latter, it should be noted that, albeit the 'feminine' lies at the root of the word 'music' itself (I.1), the participation of women in musical life is poorly attested (at least in literary sources) and the evidence often intertwines with an ideological approach, which tends to marginalize their contribution and reflect the social and power dynamics within contemporary culture (see especially De Simone 2020, with further bibliography).[26] A striking example is the stereotyped treatment of female musicians, especially pipe-players (*aulētrides*) who, from the mid sixth century BCE onwards, regularly participated in Athenian symposia (IV.2), i.e. rituals conceived as a privilege of the aristocratic male elite (Rocconi 2006; De Simone 2008). These women were courtesans (*hetairai*), hired for their artistic performances as well as for their erotic entertainment, who attended regular schools in Athens called *auletridōn didaskaleia* ('training schools of female pipe-players'); in one of his last orations, *Antidosis* 287, Isocrates (436–338 BCE) blames young citizens who spend their time there, 'wasting their youth [...] in soft living and childish folly' (transl. Norlin 1929). The expense for these musicians was one of the first budget items of a drinking party, which on some occasions became particularly high, according to the evidence we have of attempts to fix their maximum wages to not more than two drachmas (Aristotle, *Constitution of the Athenians* 50.2). Despite the disapproval of these figures and of their participation in symposia by some contemporaries,[27] the hetaeras-musicians gained so much popularity that they became stock characters in anecdotal writings as well as in Middle (*c.* 400–320 BCE) and New Comedy (320–mid third century BCE), where stylized representations of existing social categories were very common. Several comic plays – all dated between the fourth and the third century BCE – featuring these female musicians as title roles are named in the sources (unfortunately we have only fragments of them): *Aulētris* or *Aulētrides* ('pipe-player/s': Antiphanes, fr. 50 KA; Diodorus of Sinope, fr. 1 KA; Menander, fr. 64 and 66 KA; Phoenicides, fr. 1 KA), *Kitharistria* ('lyre-player': Anaxandrides, fr. 24 KA), *Psaltria* ('harp-player': Dromo, fr. 1 and 2 KA), *Orchēstris* ('dancer': Alexis, fr. 172 KA).[28] In a surviving comedy by Menander (*c.* 342–291 BCE), titled *The Arbitration*, one character (Habroton) is several times referred to as a *psaltria* and represented as the typical 'hooker with a heart of gold'. This stereotype seems to have emerged on the Greek stage to then become a stock character in Roman *palliata* (e.g. Thais in the *Eunuchus*, by the Roman playwright Terence (*c.* 190–159 BCE): Christenson 2013) as well as in modern theatrical plays and movies, up to very recent times: see, e.g., the characters Violetta Valéry in Giuseppe Verdi's *La Traviata* (1853) and Satine in Baz Luhrmann' *Moulin Rouge!* (2001).

If we turn to the topic of ethnicity, we find a similar handling of historical data. Originally, ethnic markers simply connected musical tunings, rhythms and instruments with their geographic regions of provenance (Panegyres 2007), also beyond the Greek-speaking world

(Franklin 2020); but they were soon manipulated to meet the demands of a political or cultural agenda (Rocconi 2019b; Griffith 2020). Ancient Hellenic peoples discovered their common identity as Greeks mainly through their confrontation with Persia, their principal Other, inaugurating what would become the long-lasting East–West dichotomy. Indeed, it is especially in the period of the Persian Wars, a series of conflicts which occurred between 499 and 449 BCE between the Persian Empire and many Greek *poleis*, that qualifications such as *womanish* (in a derogatory sense) and *lascivious* were frequently applied to the musical paradigm of the East,[29] in clear contrast to the austerity of the so-called genuinely Greek musical prototype (a highly artificial idea, designed to conform and respond to cultural expectations).[30]

Lydians and Phrygians were obviously non-Greek ethnic groups and viewed as such in antiquity. Nonetheless, in the seventh and sixth centuries BCE, the Lydian (divided into three variants: Mixolydian, Tense and Relaxed Lydian)[31] and the Phrygian scales (*harmoniai*) were quoted, without any implied prejudice, alongside the Dorian, Ionian or Aeolian ones (corresponding to the three main Hellenic sub-groups) as the melodic idioms most frequently used by travelling musicians living in a mobile and multicultural society. In such a society, indeed, there were plenty of cultural interactions between Greek and non-Greek people.[32] The reputation of the Lydian musical style for *softness*, perceived as potentially dangerous for the character of those who were exposed to it, seems rather to coincide with the diffusion of an unfriendly attitude towards the Ionian-Lydian customs conspicuously introduced into Athens after the creation of the Delian League, in 478 BCE.[33] In a fragment of the Athenian comic poet Cratinus (*c.* 519–422 BCE), a *didaskalos* (i.e. 'instructor') of tragic choruses – a certain Gnesippus – is mocked because of 'his chorus of hair-plucking slave women, who pluck their ugly songs [*mele*, which also mean 'limbs'] in the Lydian mode' (fr. 276 KA, transl. Storey 2011). It is precisely between the fifth and the fourth centuries BCE that Lydia became implicitly connected with the acoustics of the orientalizing symposium and therefore assigned negative stereotypes: in the *Republic* (3.398e), Plato labels the Lydian – together with the Ionian – scales as 'soft (*malakai*) and suitable for drinking parties (*sympotikai*)', as well as 'relaxed' (*chalarai*). Also the Ionian *harmonia*, though linked with one of the two main ethnic subdivisions according to which ancient Greeks categorized themselves, was itself gradually involved in this process of ideological contamination by oriental influences. This was attributed, in particular, to some Ionian colonies of the Western coasts of Anatolia, such as Miletus. In a manifestly prejudiced passage on musical *harmoniai*, the philosopher Heraclides of Pontus attributes the degeneration of the Ionian mode to the fact that 'the great majority of the Ionians have been contaminated (*ēlloiōtai*) through adaptation to the various barbarians who ruled them' (fr. 114, transl. Schütrumpf et al. 2008). As an example of this growing evidence for the proverbial association of Ionic musical style with softness, we may recall the nickname of the famous mid-fifth-century citharode, Phrynis, who was mocked as *iōnokamptēs* by his rivals (literally, 'one who sings with Ionic modulation', see Plutarch, *On Praising Oneself Inoffensively* 539c); or we might mention what Aristophanes says in *The Assembly Women* (390 BCE), where saucy songs sung by prostitutes are described as Ionic (882f.: 'Ye Muses, come sit on my lips, and find me some spicy Ionian tune', transl. Henderson 2002). Analogous remarks are usually made regarding the Phrygian paradigm. Phrygia is the land where the satyr Marsyas comes from. In a myth which became popular in the mid-fifth century BCE, Marsyas picked up the aulos thrown away by the goddess Athena (who had 'invented' it, cf. I.1) and challenged Apollo, singing to his kithara, in a musical competition (Figure 10). The Muses judged the contest, declared Apollo the winner and, as a result, the satyr was flayed and his skin hung up in a temple in Celaenae, a Phrygian town in south-western Asia Minor (the earliest reference to the story is in Herodotus (*c.* 484–415 BCE), who explicitly ascribes it to the Phrygians, see *Histories*

7.26.3). The popularity of this subject in classical art and literature may be explained in various ways, but it certainly reflects an ideological antithesis: it pitches Apollo (described as the quintessential Greek god) against Marsyas (a satyr, half-human and half-beast, coming from a foreign land like Phrygia), suggesting in turn the superiority of singing to the accompaniment of the Greek kithara over instrumental performances on the (supposedly) Asiatic aulos. The strategic and intentional opposition of Greek and Asiatic musical elements (which are sometimes alluded to in a vague and elusive way and therefore difficult to identify, as in the case of the supposed Phrygian foundation of the traditional aulos repertoire) finds, then, an explicit echo in some mythical tales and proves to have been very effective in antiquity for the construction of Hellenic identity.[34]

Figure 10 The musical contest between Apollo and Marsyas. Renaissance bronze plaquette, cast after an ancient gem, from the Medici collection (fifteenth century CE): New York (USA), Metropolitan Museum 1986.319.8.

Music also played an important part in the construction and negotiation of the national identity of modern Greece (Holst-Warhaft 2002; Tambakaki et al. 2020). When fighting for independence from Ottoman (Turkish) rule and in the process of establishing a modern state, the Greeks distanced themselves from anything that seemed oriental in their culture and sought an unbroken tradition with an idealized past. This process started in the circles of Greek emigration to Europe in the early nineteenth century and went on when a growing European idealization of classical Greece – and the consequent widespread philhellenism – encouraged the movements for Greece's independence, which was finally realized and internationally recognized in 1830. In the twentieth century, the strong belief in the continuity of a *Greek identity* across the centuries found a fundamental support in music. It was first of all encouraged by scholars of folklore (e.g. Nikolaos Politis, 1852–1921, Professor of Mythology at the University of Athens, in 1914 published a *Selections from the Songs of the Greek people* which identified folk songs as a living repository of national memory: Politis 2010 [1871]) and later reinforced by important Greek and European ethnomusicologists. To name but two, Samuel Baud-Bovy (1906–86, who between 1954 and 1973 carried out a systematic survey of the musical heritage of Crete)[35] and Thrasybulos Georgiades (1907–77, author of *Der griechische Rhythmus. Musik, Reigen, Vers und Sprache*, Hamburg 1949) repeatedly celebrated an alleged influence of ancient Greek music on neo-Greek folk music, even when the latter showed an indisputable link with Ottoman tradition. This phenomenon had an interesting (albeit on a smaller scale) parallel in early twentieth-century Italy, when a neo-romantic view of the continuity between Magna Graecia and southern Italy led Hellenists such as Ettore Romagnoli (see Introduction) to identify echoes of Greek melodies and rhythms in the Sicilian popular songs. In those years, this folk repertoire had been the subject of an attempt at recovery from the pioneer of ethnomusicology Alberto

Favara (1863–1923), who had formulated the first proposal of phylogeny of Sicilian musical folklore by hypothesizing a link with the classical tradition (Casali 2022).[36]

The most important modern musician who, throughout his entire career, emphasized such a belief in the survival of a Greek identity across the centuries is the composer Mikis Theodorakis (1925–2021), who has made Greek music famous around the world by reinterpreting the traditional folk repertoire (e.g. the *rebetika*, whose rhythms and melodies have often been incorporated in his compositions)[37] and by setting to music the verses of the most important Greek contemporary poets (as in the song cycle *Epitaphios*, on the verses of Giannis Ritsos, 1909–90, whose reception contributed to establish the image of modern Greece as 'a country of bards': Tambakaki 2019, 63). Especially during the military dictatorship of the Colonels (from 1967 to 1974), when his music was banned by the regime, Theodorakis became a symbol of freedom and resistance, playing an important role in shaping modern Greek national identity and breaking down the barriers between *art* and *popular* music with what he called *entechno laiko tragoudi*, i.e. 'art-popular song' (Holst-Warhaft 1980; Mouyis 2010; Tambakaki 2019). His insistence on the continuity of the Hellenic tradition from antiquity to the present (Theodorakis 1982, 116: in his words, modern Greek music conveys the 'essence of our tradition which ultimately comes from Byzantium and antiquity') finds concrete support in the works more openly inspired by classical antiquity, as the scores for the production of ancient dramas, i.e. *Medea* (1991), *Electra* (1995) and *Antigone* (1999), a trilogy completed by the comedy *Lysistrata* (2002), where his conscious use of melodic schemes typical of ancient Greek music (i.e., the tetrachord technique, already explored in the years 1954–60)[38] is more clearly evident, and in the formulation of his concept of Universal Harmony, which he conceived as a modern reaffirmation of the Pythagorean theories that informed all the achievements of ancient Greek art (Theodorakis 2007, esp. 85f.).

4. The construction of the public self

Among the most powerful public speeches of the beginning of the twenty-first century is the one that Barack Obama addressed to supporters after the New Hampshire presidential primary, in January 2008, when he first introduced the memorable slogan 'Yes, we can!'. Barack Obama is famous worldwide for his excellent public speaking; his speeches have been carefully studied and analysed by experts in rhetoric and political science as regards their content and rhetorical tools (logical reasoning, metaphors, repetitions and so on). But equally important is his ability to effectively modulate and adapt his voice, pauses and gestures to the message he wishes to convey (Leith 2011). In recent years, the importance of voice and gesture in securing persuasive communication in public speaking has been at the centre of research in modern Behavioural Sciences and Communication Studies (see, e.g., Mohan 2019) and it is certainly among the most successful topics of leadership consultants. It is well known that traditional rhetorical theory began in Greek and Roman times; almost every handbook on public speaking has at least one chapter on norms and precepts derived from Aristotle or Cicero. Yet few realize that, in antiquity, the theory of delivery (*hypokrisis* in Greek, *actio* or *pronuntiatio* in Latin) was contiguous with music theory, as both dealt with voice and body as means of communication. Long before Renaissance and especially Baroque aesthetics rediscovered the natural alliance of music with the verbal arts, *rhetorikē* and *mousikē technē* used the same vocabulary and concepts to describe the audible and visual abilities of their performers.

For us, rhetorical theory begins with Aristotle, but its origins were certainly earlier; see Aristotle, *The Art of Rhetoric* 1.1354a11ff.: 'At this point, previous compilers of "Arts" of rhetoric have worked out only a small portion of this art' (transl. Freese, rev. by Striker 2020).[39] Much of Aristotle's text is dedicated to the study of the logical means of persuasion (which are closed to syllogisms but, in the domain of public speech, are called enthymemes, see especially Book 1 and 2) and to the knowledge of human emotions and characters (essential to modulate the speech according to the specific audience to which it is addressed, cf. the extensive discussion in Book 2). In Book 3, the focus shifts to style and delivery. The latter is 'of the greatest importance, but has not yet been treated of by any one' (*The Art of Rhetoric* 3.1403b), probably because it draws on nature rather than art – hence the difficulty in formulating a theory of it (3.1404a15–18). Poetry and rhetoric, Aristotle says, are both acoustic experiences, since actors, rhapsodists and rhetoricians all use the voice (*phōnē*) to communicate. Music and language share intensity, pitch and temporal organization of acoustic signals, also in virtue of the fact that ancient Greek had a pitch accent and was based on syllable lengths (Devine and Stephens 1994; see also I.2, esp. n. 25). Therefore, the means through which the human voice may arouse different emotions in the hearer are volume (*megethos*), melodic design (*harmonia*) and rhythmical patterns (*rhythmos*):

> Now delivery is a matter of voice (*phōnē*), as to the mode in which it should be used for each particular emotion; when it should be loud (*megalē*), when low (*mikra*), when intermediate (*mesē*); and how the tones (*tonoi*), that is, shrill (*oxeisa*), deep (*bareia*), and intermediate (*mesē*), should be used; and what rhythms (*rhythmoi*) are adapted to each subject. For there are three qualities that are considered, volume (*megethos*), harmony (*harmonia)*, rhythm (*rhythmos*) [...] in every system of instruction there is some slight necessity to pay attention to style; for it does make a difference, for the purpose of making a thing clear, to speak in this or that manner; still, the difference is not so very great, but all these things are mere outward show for pleasing the hearer (*pros ton akroatēn*).
>
> Aristotle, *The Art of Rhetoric* 3.1403b26–1404a11, transl. Freese, rev. by Striker 2020

The existence of a theoretical reflection on the basic elements of language (which the ancients called *prosōidia*, i.e. 'prosody', *pros* + *ōidē*, lit. 'towards the song') and of a technical vocabulary capable of indicating the key features of Greek *phōnē* is attested from the late fifth century BCE. Its origin can be traced back to those discussions in which exponents of technical fields, the so-called sophists (cf. I.3), claimed competence over a specific *technē*: 'Well, then, those matters which you (sc. the sophist Hippias of Elis) of all men know best how to discuss, concerning the value of letters and syllables and rhythms and harmonies' (Plato, *Greater Hippias* 285c–d, transl. North Fowler 1926).[40] Still later handbooks, such as Pseudo-Demetrius' *On Style* (probably written between the first century BCE and the first century CE), point out the shared terminology between the two areas of concern: '*Mousikoi* (music theorists?)[41] speak of words as smooth, rough, well proportioned, and weighty' (*On Style* 176, transl. Innes and Rhys Roberts 1995). After Aristotle, his pupil and successor as head of the Lyceum Theophrastus of Eresus (371–287 BCE), author of several works on rhetoric and music, was probably the first who developed an independent treatment of delivery, which for Aristotle was still subordinated to style. Theophrastus influenced the recognition of delivery as the fourth part of rhetoric (with style, invention and arrangement)[42] by writing a special work *On Delivery* (now lost), where he extended the meaning of the term *hypokrisis* from voice to bodily movements (fr. 712 FHS&G, see Fortenbaigh 2003, esp. 271). He also paid attention to the euphonic properties of language: 'Charm in style also comes from what are called beautiful words. According to the definition of Theophrastus, beauty in a word is that which gives pleasure to the ear or the eye, or has an inherent nobility of thought' (fr. 687 FHS&G, transl. Innes and Rhys Roberts 1995). After him, more and more attention was paid to the aural attributes of speech. The strongest and most specific interest in euphony was carried out by the so-called *kritikoi*, Hellenistic literary critics who posited the faculty of hearing as the supreme arbiter of excellence.[43]

The theorization process on the role and the power of delivery in oratorical performances found its full completion when it moved to Rome. Roman authors discussed voice, countenance, gesture and their persuasive effect on the listeners at length (Schülz 2020): the most famous among them are the anonymous writer of the *Rhetoric to Gaius Herennium* (late 80s BCE) and the orator Cicero (106–43 BCE) who, especially in *On the Orator* (55 BCE), *Brutus* and *The Orator* (both of 46 BCE), focused on the properties of the voice (volume, stability and flexibility) and on the different tones that should be used in delivery, described as 'the dominant factor of oratory' (Cicero, *On the Orator* 3.213, transl. Rackham 1942).[44] But the work in which the ancient bond between rhetoric and music is more emphasized is *The Orator's Education* of Marcus Fabius Quintilianus (late first century CE). In line with the pedagogical project of his treatise, Quintilian underlines the fundamental role that music must play in the education of the youth and mentions the musical training that orators must follow with the grammarians, vocal trainers and theatrical actors, while respecting the specifics: while learning how to read poetic texts, the future orator should not modulate his voice to the point of turning it into song, grace in movement should never lead to an excessive artificiality of gestures and so on (*The Orator's Education* 1.8.2, 1.11.19, 1.12.3, 11.3.89 and *passim*: cf. Hall 2007; Melidis 2020). Referring explicitly to Greek musical sources (i.e. Aristoxenus, quoted in 1.10.22–3), Quintilian recognizes equal importance to the voice and the body, saying that the one appeals to the eye, the other to the ear, 'the two senses by which all emotion penetrates to the mind' (11.3.14), and dedicates the greatest part of an entire book (Book 11) to delivery. Here he deals quite extensively with gestures (from 11.3.65 to 11.3.136), to which he attributes an explicit and precise meaning that is independent of the words they accompany, focusing especially on arms (11.3.83–84), hands (11.3.85–87) and finger positions (11.3.92–106). This interest in describing the finer details of a whole range of expressive hand and finger poses (11.3.179), which 'speak for themselves' (*ipsae locuntur*, 11.3.86) and without which delivery is rendered 'mutilated and ineffective' (*trunca* [...] *ac debilis,* 11.385), was absolutely new in rhetorical sources and laid the foundations for the future development of a taxonomy of gesture (Hall 2004).[45] It would become highly influential in later times (Cox 2021), both in the Middle Ages (when hand gesture and its depiction served as a sort of universal language for illiterate people) and especially in the Renaissance (in the wake of the rediscovery in 1416 of a complete manuscript of Quintilian's treatise at the Swiss abbey of St Gall by the humanist Poggio Bracciolini, 1380–1459),[46] when gesture also attracted the interest of visual artists and theorists of painting (e.g. Leon Battista Alberti's *On Painting*, 1435–6).

Conclusions: Looking Ahead

Beyond the myth

The journey through history we have taken so far has shown how persistent, albeit varied, the legacy of Greek *mousikē* has been in Western culture. The numerous examples of uses and revivals, reimagination and rewriting of such an ideal have allowed us to formulate some hypotheses concerning the possible reasons behind its lasting attraction over time: from the pursuit of an authoritative example for musical experiments of various kinds (as those inspired by the antiquarian studies of Renaissance and Baroque musical theorists: II.1–2) to the search for a cultural legitimacy of new theories or compositional forms (e.g. the modes of medieval plainchant or the theatrical genre of melodrama: II.1) or for a model to be surpassed (as in the denial of the traditional mimetic paradigm by musical formalism: III.2–3); from the ideological manipulation of ancient ideas for propagandizing purposes (such as that deployed in the construction of modern Hellenic identity: IV.3) to the nostalgic restoration or revival in performance of an idealized past (e.g. Palmer Sikelianos' project to re-enact the multimedia of ancient Greek drama in the modern world: see Introduction). Whatever the reason, Western perceptions of classical antiquity have certainly influenced the European cultural history of music to a great extent, acting as a medium of change or continuity as well as contributing to shape musical repertoires and to affect intellectual discussions over the centuries. But can the ideas and practices of ancient *mousikē* still have a role in the contemporary world, decontextualized from their historical setting?

In recent years, given the interdisciplinary nature of the topic, scholars with an interest in ancient *mousikē* have felt the need to collaborate more intensely with each other, hence encouraging the creation of societies and study-groups that connected academics with different expertise (such as the International Society for the Study of Greek and Roman Music and its Cultural Heritage, better known as MOISA). This cooperation has led scholars to refine their knowledge in the field; the consequent dissemination of data, ideas and proposals have increasingly stimulated the interest of classicists, musicologists, philosophers, psychologists and anthropologists (and many others) in this until recently neglected area of research (for a summary of the latest advancements of the discipline, see Rocconi and Lynch 2020). The communication among people in different fields has been facilitated by the growing availability of new translations and commentaries of important theoretical works or fragmentary texts (starting from the material collected by Barker 1984 and 1989, which finally made available sources that, until then, had been the prerogative and interest of only a few initiates), as well as by the publication of handbooks and companions (e.g. West 1992; Mathiesen 1999; Lynch and Rocconi 2020), which have all contributed, and are still contributing, to bring the experts into mutual dialogue with critical debates across other academic disciplines.

Beyond this, thanks to modern technology, the study and evaluation of material finds (i.e. musical instruments) and acoustic environments (especially theatres) – the privileged object of investigation of relatively new disciplines such as music archaeology and archaeoacustics – have greatly advanced modern understanding of timbres, pitches, sounds and scales used in the music of ancient times (see especially Hagel 2010), helping convert the data inferred from the findings into audible information and supporting the construction of good replicas (both actual and virtual) on a much more scientific basis (see, e.g., Hagel 2004 and 2012; Psaroudakēs 2013 and 2020;

Psaroudakēs et al. 2021; Terzēs 2013 and 2020; Bellia 2021; for a detailed survey of these latest tendencies in scholarship, see Hagel 2022). These new discoveries and in-depth analysis have necessarily increased our awareness of the historical distance that separates us from the ancients, allowing modern scholars to overcome, as far as possible, the musical *antiquarianism* that has characterized the approach to antiquity in other times of history (on the inevitability that reconstructions of the past would be 'inherently revisions' of it, see the interesting remarks in Dorf 2019, esp. 7–34). At the same time, however, this breakthrough has never ceased to stimulate the creativity of contemporary musicians and composers, as has always happened in the past whenever striking discoveries were announced (see the examples quoted throughout the book). The last decades have, in fact, seen an incredible proliferation of activities of individual performers and groups as well as composers, sometimes personally involved in research activities, who, by drawing inspiration from new developments in scientific knowledge, now animate museum itineraries, educational activities, theatrical and film projects, exploiting the internet and spreading their performances on the web (cf. the 'Suggestions for Further Reading'). These historically informed events, which sometimes claim to restore things to an *original* state (hence echoing the assumptions behind the revival of other early music traditions in the nineteenth and twentieth centuries, cf. Haines 2013), are not always easily appealing to the general public and sometimes presuppose a thorough understanding of the scientific criteria underlying performance (on the dangers inherent in revivalism, see Brook 1968). Nevertheless, they all show a creative component that is revitalizing the role of the Classics in the academic field and, at the same time, attests to the *liveliness* of the research topic of ancient Greek music well beyond strictly scholarly purposes.

Suggestions for Further Reading

General

The most comprehensive bibliography on ancient Greek music and its legacy, up to 1999, is in Mathiesen 1999, 699–783. Titles from 2000 onwards have increased exponentially in the last twenty years, due to the growing interest in music-related aspects of Greek and Roman culture: they are regularly listed in the online bibliography 'De musicis' on the website of MOISA: The International Society for the Study of Greek and Roman Music and its Cultural Heritage (https://www.moisasociety.org/bibliography). Since 2013 the scholarly literature on the subject has been enriched with contributions from the specialist periodical *Greek and Roman Musical Studies*. Two further journals more narrowly focused on music archaeology, a discipline whose results have proved to be pivotal for reconstructions of ancient Greek and Roman music and musical instruments, deal often – although not exclusively – with music in classical antiquity: the *Journal of Music Archaeology* and *TELESTES: An International Journal of Archaeomusicology and Archaeology of Sound*. The former continues the spirit of *Studien zur Musikarchäologie*, the book series which since 2000 has published the proceeding of the *ISGMA* conferences (*International Study-Group on Music Archaeology*); the latter is linked to a series of books on the same topic (*TELESTES: Studi e ricerche di archeologia musicale nel Mediterraneo*), whose aim is the valorization of the ancient musical heritage in the Mediterranean. An online catalogue of musical findings of the Mediterranean area, now preserved in museums, is currently under construction as an Italian-French project entitled *RIMAnt: Repertorium Instrumentorum Musicorum Antiquorum*: https://www.hisoma.mom.fr/recherche-et-activites/2021-2025/b1-rimant.

The best handbook still in use as a general introduction to ancient Greek music is West 1992 (Landels 1999 and Mathiesen 1999 are out of date; Hagel 2010 is excellent but rather technical; Klavan 2021 is a nice survey but much more restricted in scope). The most up-to-date work of synthesis on the topic is Lynch and Rocconi 2020, which contains thirty-four chapters covering the most significant issues in the field and provides specific bibliographic references on each of them.

The primary sources on music theory and thought (most of which are collected in Jan 1962 [1895]) started to be more widely accessible some decades ago thanks to the English translations in Barker 1984 and 1989: the first of these two volumes gathers together the most important passages in Greek literature describing musical activities, the contexts of their performance and the educational value of *mousikē*; the second volume offers the most complete collection of writings on harmonic and acoustic theory ever translated into English. To these texts, new translations, critical editions and commentaries on lesser-known works or fragmentary texts have been added in the following years and are constantly increasing. The standard collection of documentary evidence of ancient theoretical knowledge on music is still Mathiesen 1988. In the 1990s, the same author also established the online *Thesaurus Musicarum Latinarum* (TML), which includes every known Latin text on music theory from late antiquity to the seventeenth century (https://chmtl.indiana.edu/tml/).

The most complete and up-to-date collection of extant melodies and fragments is Pöhlmann and West 2001 (*DAGM*), which replaced the pioneering collection of Pöhlmann 1970. An online critical edition of the ancient Greek musical documents is now under construction thanks to the *DIAGRAM* project (*Digitising Aspects of Graphical Representation in Ancient Music*) hosted by the Austrian Academy of Sciences (https://www.oeaw.ac.at/en/oeai/oeaidigital/laufende-projekte/webplattformen-forschungstools/diagram-digitising-aspects-of-graphical-representation-in-ancient-music).

Reception

A selection of the most important publications concerning the issues discussed in the book has been quoted in each chapter and listed in the main Bibliography. On reception of ancient Greek and Roman music there is no comprehensive volume: contributions on individual topics are listed in the online bibliography 'De musicis' cited above. To name but a few: on dance see Hall and Wyles 2008; Delavaud-Roux 2019; Gianvittorio-Ungar and Schlapbach 2021. On reinterpretations of ancient musical myths and themes in iconography: Castaldo 2009, 2012, 2018 and 2020; Guidobaldi 2007 and 2020; Rodríguez López and Romero Mayorga 2019; Young 2020. On the legacy of the idea of cosmic harmony: Hicks 2017; Prins and Vanhaelen 2018. On reception of ancient classical themes in Renaissance culture, see, e.g., Palisca 1985 and 1989; Restani 1990, 2001, 2011a, 2011b, 2012, 2015, 2019b, 2020. On the music of the late nineteenth and twentieth centuries: Solomon 2010 and 2016; Dorf 2019 and 2021; Levidou, Romanou and Vlastos 2016. On classics and opera, the bibliography is huge: in addition to the titles already quoted throughout the book, see Napolitano 2010; Solomon 2013; Ketterer and Solomon 2017. Among the online resources, it is worth mentioning the *Archive of Performance of Greek and Roman Drama* (*APGRD*: http://www.apgrd.ox.ac.uk/), which collects a wide range of archival, digital and bibliographic resources about the reception of ancient theatrical texts, including in a musical context.

Reconstructions

In recent years, several reperformances and reconstructions of ancient music have been attempted by scholars in the field of music archaeology or by performers themselves involved in research activities. Among the academics: Annie Bélis (CNRS), founder of one of the first modern groups to perform ancient music on replicas of ancient instruments, the *Ensemble Kérylos* (see below); Stefan Hagel (Austrian Academy of Sciences), who has frequently demonstrated his scholarly work to an international public audience in form of lecture-concerts; John C. Franklin (University of Vermont), who has widely experimented with the historically informed composition of music for ancient Greek tragedies and comedies (Franklin 2002b and 2019); Stelios Psaroudakēs (National & Kapodistrian University of Athens), very active in complementing his research work with public musical performances on the lyre; Chrēstos Terzēs (Austrian Academy of Sciences), who built several replicas of musical archaeological findings to integrate his research activity; Armand D'Angour (University of Oxford), who, on the basis of the famous papyrus fragment of Euripides' *Orestes*, created a score that has become part of a widely viewed YouTube video presentation of a performance in Oxford (D'Angour 2021); Tosca A. C. Lynch (University of Oxford), founder of the digital project *eMousikē: Ancient Greek music online* (https://www.emousike.com/); Anna Conser (Columbia University), who has applied her research work on accentual melodies to the production of a Greek tragedy mounted by Barnard Columbia Ancient Drama (Conser 2020; Power 2020); Athena Katsanevaki (Aristotle University of Thessaloniki), an ethnomusicologist who combines the study of ancient music with fieldwork in the traditional singing of modern Greece (Katsanevaki 2017 and 2023).

Many are the instrument builders, composers, performers and musical groups who, in recent years, have been active in promoting the knowledge of ancient Greek and Roman music in various contexts and have given a contemporary voice to ancient instruments. To name but a few: Gregorio Paniagua and the *Atrium Musicae de Madrid*, who, back in the late 1970s, published the first modern recording in which ancient Greek musical documents were performed (https://

web.archive.org/web/20100323063724/http://usuarios.multimania.es/ gregoriopaniagua/); the French *Ensemble Kérylos* (http://www. kerylos.fr/en/); Conrad Steinmann and the *Ensemble Melpomen* (https://www.melpomen.ch/site/en/home-2/ensemble/); the Italian groups *Synaulia* (https://www.soundcenter.it/synaulia.htm) and *Ludi scaenici* (http://www.ludi-scaenici.it/ludeng.html); the German ensemble *Musica romana* (http://www.musica-romana.de/de/index-beta.html); the Greek composer, trumpet and lyre player Nikos Xanthoulis, who has revived the practice and teaching of the ancient Greek seven-stringed lyre and written incidental music for tragedies performed in Greece and abroad (https://www.nikosxanthoulis. com/); the Hellenic musical ensemble *Orphean Harmony*, an entire orchestra which studies and re-imagines the music of Greek antiquity (https://luxgreekevents.wordpress.com/orphean-harmony/); the pipe-player, producer and lecturer Barnaby Brown (https://barnabybrown. info/); the performer and composer Callum Armstrong (https:// callumarmstrong.co.uk/); the expert on brass instruments of ancient Europe Peter Holmes, who has recently started a series of publications on the topic (https://www.hornandtrumpet.com/); the instrument maker and player, specializing in the Roman hydraulic organ, Justus Willberg (http://www.emaproject.eu/justus-willberg. html); the composer Mary Ann Tedstone Glover (https://www. maryanntedstoneglover.com/).

Notes

Chapter 1

1   On the notion of *prōtos heurētēs*, see Baumbach 2006; Wessels and
    Klooster 2022. The term *heuretēs* ('discoverer', rather than 'inventor')
    derives from the verb *heuriskein* ('to find') and its usage implies a
    poetics of imitation rather than a creative approach to artistic
    production (Gentili 1988, 54ff.).

2   While commenting on Alcman's famous fr. 39 Page (seventh century
    BCE, 'These words and melody Alcman *found* – from *heuriskein* – by
    putting into words the tongued cry of partridges'), Athenaeus of
    Naucratis (second–third century CE) reports that, according to the
    Peripatetic philosopher Chamaeleon of Pontus (fourth–third century
    BCE), music's discovery was devised by the ancients 'from the birds
    singing in lonely places' (*Sophists at Dinner* 9.389f–390a).

3   On 'Muse' as 'song', see Pindar, *Pythian* 5.65; Plato, *Laws* 2.668b5 and
    670a4. Cf. Halliwell 2011, 58: 'The Muses are internalized in and
    inseparable from the workings of song (they *are* the essence of song,
    which came into existence with their "birth") in a way which makes
    them different from the status of many other deities'.

4   The educational value of *mousikē* is implied, e.g., in Aristophanes,
    Knights 188f., transl. Henderson 1998a: 'Look, mister, I'm uneducated
    (*oude mousikēn epistamai*, lit. 'I do not know *mousikē*') except for
    reading and writing, and I'm damn poor even at those'. A useful survey
    of the values attached to this cultural notion and its opposite *amousia* is
    in Halliwell 2012.

5   The Muses first appear in Greek literature in the *Iliad* (1.595–604),
    where they sing at the feast of the gods on Mount Olympus responding
    to Apollo's performance on the lyre. The connection of individual
    Muses with different poetic genres or sciences (Calliope with epic
    poetry, Ourania with astronomy, etc.) was developed in the Hellenistic
    period and became systematic only in Roman imperial culture,

facilitating their identification as personifications of the liberal arts in the Middle Ages.

6   Greatly different conceptions of music have been developed by the world's societies. Some cultures do not even have a single word for music and discuss it by reference to individual genres or types, see Nettl 2001, with further bibliography.

7   On the concept of social construction, see Berger and Luckmann 1966. The idea of musical autonomy, i.e. regarded as free from historical and social contingencies, was dominant in twentieth-century discussions on Western art music, but has been recently called into question, see Clarke 2011.

8   This list culminates with the Muse Calliope, reserving the place of honour to the singing voice (that is, to musical poetry), the most distinguished genre of music in antiquity. A similar prominent position is given to Calliope on the François Vase (570 BCE), see Figure 2.

9   *Choros* here means 'place for choral dancing and singing' (as in *Iliad* 18.590 and *Odyssey* 8.260). Only later would the term metonymically assume the meaning 'band of dancers and singers'.

10 In other sources, the poet is described as a 'prophet' of the Muses: cf. Pindar, *Paean* 6.6 and fr. 150.

11 For a re-evaluation of the senses and matter in the construction of ancient aesthetic thought, see especially Porter 2010; Peponi 2012 (cf. III.1).

12 As the occurrence of the term *technē* well demonstrates, the modern separation between practical technique and artistic activity does not fit the Greek notion of *mousikē*.

13 See, e.g., Aristotle, *Metaphysics* 1.981b7–9, transl. Tredennick 1933: 'In general the sign of knowledge or ignorance is the ability to teach, and for this reason we hold that art (*technē*) rather than experience is scientific knowledge (*epistēmē*); for the artists can teach, but the others cannot'.

14 These musicians/theorists, who based their inquiry into musical sounds on hearing, are elsewhere labelled as *harmonikoi*, i.e. 'experts in the study of *harmonia*': Aristoxenus, *Elements of Harmonics* 2.25–30; Theophrastus (*c.* 370/1–279 BCE), *Characters* 10 and fr. 716.17–18 FHS&G; P.Hibeh 1.13 (*c.* fourth century BCE).

15 Cf. Hesychius *s* 1371: '*sophistēs*: They referred to every *technē* as *sophia*, and as *sophistai* to those who spend their time on *mousikē* and sing along to the lyre'.

16 On the cultural assumptions behind this approach, see Becker 1986.

17 In extant Greek literature, we find two verbs derived from the same root as *mousikē*, both rarely attested (five occurrences for the first, thirteen for the second): the oldest of them is *mousizein* ('to sing' or 'to play'), firstly used by the poet Euripides (480–406 BCE) to indicate the bad performance of a drunk Cyclops (Euripides, *Cyclops* 489); the other is *mousikeuesthai* ('to cultivate a taste for music'), which appears for the first time in fr. 83b of the historian Duris of Samos (*c.* 350–281) to describe the passion for music of the mythical hero Amphion (one of the twin sons of Antiope and Zeus, who had received a lyre as a gift from the god Hermes).

18 The first mention of the existence of *parasemantikē* (lit. 'the art of placing symbols along') is in Aristoxenus, *Elements of Harmonics* 39.20–2 (late fourth century BCE), but the earliest surviving examples on papyrus are from the third century BCE (*DAGM* 3 and 4).

19 The primacy of musical *works* (in sharp opposition with *events*) in the history of music was strongly advocated by the musicologist Carl Dahlhaus (1928–89, see Dahlhaus 1983 [1977]), who has exerted a strong influence on modern musicology. On the origins of the 'work concept' in Western art music, see Butt 2015.

20 The terms *mousikē* and *choreia* occur together in *Laws* 2.654c, where they seem to be used as a hendiadic pair: 'this sort of man that is better educated in the choric art and in music' (*tēn choreian te kai mousikēn*).

21 According to Plato, good melodies (*melē*) and dances (*schēmata*) may train the soul towards virtues, thanks to their mimetic character (III.3). He says that, in choric performance, there are 'representations of characters' (*mimēmata tropōn*, 2.655d5) which are realized not only through the *content* of the songs (that is, through their text), but also through their most technical and formal patterns: melodies and rhythms (669b–670c).

22 In the *Laws* (3.700a–701b, cf. IV.1), Plato gives his famous nostalgic view of the music of the past, whose types and forms were once

properly distinguished probably in order to differentiate the types of worship. As other scholars have demonstrated (e.g. Rossi 1971 and 2000), Plato's division of *mousikē* into well-defined genres has a *con-textual* (rather than strictly formal) basis, since it does not take into account the *literary* aspects of genres, but rather their performative and contextual characteristics.

23 Plato's fanciful etymology (*choreia* from *chara*, 'joy') is indicative of a feature that Plato (and probably any Greek) regarded as inherent in choral activity, as the parallelism with the Hesiodic passage clearly suggests.

24 Similarly, in *Pythian* 5.65-7 Pindar praises Apollo for providing human beings with the lyre and for 'putting peaceful good governance into their minds'.

25 In antiquity, musical rhythm and melody were deeply rooted in *logos*. Firstly, the syllabic quantities of the Greek language were clearly detectable and had a distinguishing value (long vs short). Secondly, Greek was a pitch language, i.e. syllables carrying the acute accent were pronounced at a higher pitch than the other syllables, while those carrying a circumflex accent showed a rise and a fall in pitch. This gave a melodic contour to language and offered a natural basis for creating the shape of the melody in poetry, being also of great help in memorizing ideas and information (cf. IV.4).

26 Later this approach became prominent in the so-called *book culture* of the Hellenistic period, when most poetry was no longer composed for musical performance. On the role of Aristotle's *Poetics* in this process, see especially Ford 2002 and 2015.

27 Although defining music as the greatest among tragedy's embellishments (*Poetics* 6.1450b16), Aristotle says nothing about it. For his focus on dramatic structure, see 6.1450a15ff., transl. Halliwell 1995: 'practically every drama has items of spectacle, character, plot, diction, lyric poetry, and thought, alike. *The most important of these things is the structure of events* [...] *the events and the plot are the goal of tragedy, and the goal is the most important thing of all*' (italics mine).

28 See Aristotle *Poetics* 26.1462a15-16 and *Politics* 8.1340b17.

29 The music accompanying a poetic text was based on its rhythm (i.e. metrics) and the tonal intonation of words (cf. n. 25 above); therefore it should not be understood as an ornament added at a later stage.

30 Cf. Small (1998, 163), focusing here on pure instrumental music (i.e. the sonata): 'The concept and the vocabulary of sonata form that was developed through the study of scores, though perhaps useful in a limited sense, have misled musicians into viewing synoptically, as a structure, all of whose features exist simultaneously, what is actually a series of events in time. *Structure is a static concept, carrying an implication of something permanent or at least lasting and, in the case of musical works, of something that transcends the ephemerality of performance and has nothing to do with its dynamics.* It thus inclines us to think of performance as at best contingent to the work's nature and meaning and even as irrelevant to it' (italics mine).

31 On the notion of *process* in music, see Readhead and Hawes 2016. On the close connection still existing between modern Greek poetry and oral performance, see Mackridge 2020.

32 On arts in education, see Nussbaum 2010 (esp. ch. 6: 'Cultivating Imagination: Literature and the Arts'). The thesis of this book, according to which the most important contribution of a liberal education is its ability to shape citizenry in a democracy and to help them understand their lives, has been recently challenged by Rens Bod, expert in computational linguistics and history of science (Bod, Maat and Weststeijn 2010, 2012 and 2014). By searching for principles and patterns in various disciplines within the humanities, from antiquity to the present, Bod intends to demonstrate that their primary role has rather been the elaboration of a scientific method (later fully developed by the experimental sciences), which has provided human beings with the tools to analyse the *structure* of reality.

33 In Plato's ideal city, traditional rites and religion were of fundamental importance: hence the great value he assigns to *choreia* in the *Laws* (on which see Prauscello 2014).

34 All Greek choruses were arranged according to the different phases of human life (children, girls/boys, women/men), so the main function of these ritual gatherings was accompanying the transition from one age

to the other, as well as defining the social role, age group, gender and political status of their participants.

35 In the *Clouds* (964–72, cf. IV.1), Aristophanes (*c.* 450–385 BCE) describes the old education as based on gymnastics as well as lyre training and singing (of the same author, see also *Knights* 987–96). A basic musical competence was essential in order to participate in symposia, as attested in Aristophanes' *Wasps* (1207ff.): here a character teaches his father how to be 'symposiastic' (*xympotikos*) and 'convivialistic' (*xynousiastikos*) by testing his ability to sing to the accompaniment of an aulos-player (1219ff.). On the importance of the *kitharistēs* in education: Plato, *Laws* 2.663e–666e, 7.812b–813a; *Protagoras* 326a–b.

36 For a panoramic survey of the discipline of philosophy of education, see Siegel, Phillips and Callan 2018.

37 There is no scholarly agreement on the interpretation of the term *mousikē* in Book 8 of the *Politics* (see, e.g., Ford 2004 and Jones 2012). I believe that Aristotle is here considering *mousikē* only with reference to its strictly musical aspects – which is to say as a complex of melody and rhythm – and that learning music here means learning to *perform* music, i.e. to play an instrument and to sing the right pitches in the right rhythms.

38 The model here is not Athens, where education was privately run, but rather Sparta, where it was controlled and provided by the state. On the importance of Aristotle's defence of public education in current debates about educational inclusion, see Curren 2000.

39 Cf. Plato, *Protagoras* 326a–b (where we are told that grammar is taught by a separate teacher, the *grammatistēs*), *Clitias* 407b–c, *Charmides* 159c.

40 On the notions of *to kalon* and music in Aristotle's ethics, see Gottlieb 2021 (esp. ch. 7: '*To Kalon* and Music'). On leisure (*scholē*) as the goal of a virtuous life, see also Aristotle *Nicomachean Ethics* 10.6.1177b4: 'happiness is found only in leisure' (transl. Rackham 1926).

41 Music's contribution to *phronēsis*, mentioned by Aristotle together with *diagōgē* in 8.1339a25f. ('[sc. *mousikē*] contributes to our way of living/*diagōgē* and increases our wisdom/*phronēsis*'), seems to refer to 'practical wisdom', that is, to the capacity of a man to consistently choose

what is to be done in each of the particular situations he encounters, in agreement with the ethical principles embedded in his character. For another interpretation of the term *phronēsis*, see Destrée 2017.

42 Aristotle, *Politics* 8.1340a38–1340b8: 'But melodies themselves do contain imitations (*mimēmata*) of character. This is perfectly clear, for the *harmoniai* have quite distinct natures from one another, so that those who hear them are differently affected and do not respond in the same way to each [...] with rhythms the situation is the same'. Cf. *Politics* 8.1340a28ff.: 'among the objects of the other senses there are no likenesses of character'. On the contrary, according to Plato, *Republic* 3.400a1–3, the guide of musical imitation must be assumed by the verbal components of *mousikē*.

43 This tendency seems to have found its completion in Boethius (*c.* 480–524/6 CE), who is also responsible for the adoption of the term *quadrivium* (lit. 'four-way crossroad'). Cf. Boethius, *Fundamentals of Music* 1.34, transl. Bower 1989: '*How much nobler, then, is the study of music as a rational discipline than as composition and performance* [...] But a musician is one who has gained knowledge of making music by weighing with the reason, not through the servitude of work, but through the sovereignty of speculation' (italics mine). For a reassessment of the emergence of the seven-liberal-arts curriculum in ancient education, see Hadot 2005 [1984], according to whom the *trivium/quadrivium* division was probably formalized only around the third century CE in a Neoplatonic milieu.

44 For the rediscovery of the *Politics* in the Renaissance (a text almost unknown to medieval translators and completely ignored, as far as we know, in the Arabic traditions), see Besso, Guagliumi and Pezzoli 2008. An influential promoter of this approach was the Florentine humanist Leonardo Bruni (1370–1444), who produced new translations of these Aristotelian works from the original Greek texts (1417: *Nicomachean Ethics*; 1420: *Economics*; 1436/38: *Politics*) and wrote a political treatise inspired by Aristotle's model (1439: *Sulla costituzione dei fiorentini*). Before him, the *Politics* was known in Europe only thanks to the circulation of its first Latin translation by William of Moerbeke (1215–86), made *c.* 1260 (cf. Schütrumpf 2014a).

45 This expression, which in the Renaissance assumed such a specific
    value, derives from Cicero, *For Archias* 3 and *In Defence of Murena* 61.

46 On the place of music in the medieval *quadrivium*, see Dyer 2007.

47 This work, written between 1277 and 1280, was published in Rome only
    in 1607 (Briggs 1999). It was the most successful 'mirror of princes' of
    medieval political thought, a literary genre offering a model for the
    ideal prince to follow: see especially Restani 2020, 463ff.

48 The expression *in consonantia vocum* has been interpreted as a
    reference to polyphonic music in Gallo 1995, 64.

49 In the fourteenth century, the knowledge of the *Politics* spread
    throughout Europe also thanks to the French translation by the
    philosopher Nicole Oresme, completed in 1374 (see Menut 1970).

50 Bruni's translation had actually been commissioned by the Duke
    Humfrey of Gloucester in 1433 but, before being sent to him, the author
    dedicated it to Pope Eugene IV: Hunkins 2007–8; Schütrumpf 2014b.

51 On the importance of these schools for the establishment of new
    musical chapels, see especially Gambassi 1997; Pietschmann and
    Steichen 2015. For the hypothesis that Bruni's translation of the *Politics*
    inspired Pope Eugene, see especially Gallo 1998, 121.

52 The international society that coordinates and discuss the activities and
    the different models of training in music therapy is the WFMT, 'World
    Federation of Music Therapy': https://wfmt.info/.

53 Theophrastus, fr. 726A FHS&G, transl. Fortenbaugh et al. 1992:'he (sc.
    Theophrastus) says that music cures many of the ills that affect the soul
    and the body, such as fainting, fright and prolonged disturbances of mind.
    For the playing of the aulos, he says, cures both sciatica and epilepsy'.

54 *Paian* was originally a healing god, only later equated with Apollo:
    Käppel 2006.

55 Cf. also Pratinas of Phlius (lyric and tragic poet, sixth–fifth century
    BCE), fr. 713 Page, according to whom the Cretan singer Thaletas of
    Gortyn (seventh century BCE) purified Sparta with his music, and
    Aristoxenus, fr. 117 Wehrli, who relates that an oracle from Delphi
    prescribed performances of paeans to calm the hysteria of the women
    in Locri and Rhegium, in South Italy.

56 Cf. *On the Pythagorean Way of Life* 110, transl. Dillon and Hershbell 1991: 'For he [sc. Pythagoras] accorded a major role to purification (*katharsei*) by this means. Indeed, he called this *medical treatment through music*' (italics mine).

57 Aristotle, *On the Soul* 1.1.403a16–19, transl. Hett 1957: 'Probably all the affections of the soul are associated with the body – anger, gentleness, fear, pity, courage and joy, as well as loving and hating; for *when they appear the body is also affected*' (italics mine).

58 The first two *pathē* mentioned in the *Politics* by Aristotle, pity and fear, are probably selected in order to prepare for the definition of tragedy in the *Poetics* 1449b27f., transl. Halliwell 1995: 'Tragedy, then, is mimesis of an action which is elevated [...] *through pity and fear accomplishing the catharsis of such emotion*' (italics mine).

59 The same mechanism is implicit in Plato's description of the effects of exposure to Phrygian melodies (usually arousing the *enthousiasmos*) described in Book 3 of the *Republic* (399b), i.e. restraint and moderation, even if *katharsis* is not mentioned here.

60 On the existence of two different systems of music therapy in antiquity, one allopathic and one homeopathic, see also Aristides Quintilianus (third–fourth century CE), *On Music* 2.14, transl. Barker 1989: 'If you use *harmoniai* in the ways we have explained, applying them to each soul on the basis *either* of their similarity (*kath'homoiotēta*) *or* of their opposition (*kat'enantiotēta*) to it, you will disclose the bad character that lurks within it, and cure it, and replace it with a better'.

61 The birth of the modern theory of harmony traditionally begins with the theoretical writings of the French Baroque composer Jean-Philippe Rameau, starting from his *Traité de l'harmonie* (Paris 1722).

62 On the application of the notion of 'fitting together' to musical contexts, see, e.g., Lambropoulou 1995–6; Franklin 2002a; Provenza 2014. On *harmonia* = 'octave interval', perceived as a blend of opposites, see Ps.-Aristotle, *Problems* 19.38, transl. Barker 1984: 'for diseases are movements of unnatural ordering of the body. But we enjoy concord because it is a blend of opposites that stand in ratio to each other'.

63 Cf. Heraclitus, frs 51 and 10 DK; Hippocratic *De Victu* 1.8. For the
    former of these passages, see Sassi 2015; for the latter Bartoš 2015,
    151–5; Pelosi 2016.

64 Fr. 6a DK: 'The size of *harmonia* (i.e. the octave) is *syllaba* (i.e. the
    fourth) and *di'oxeia*n (i.e. the fifth)'. For a comment on this fragment,
    see Huffmann 1993, 145–65; Barker 2007, 264–78; Rocconi 2020,
    615–18.

65 Some medical views ascribed to the Pythagorean Philolaus (provided
    by a pupil of Aristotle, Menon, fourth century BCE, *Anonymi
    Londinensis ex Aristotelis Iatricis Menoniis et aliis medicis eclogue* 18.8)
    are based on the principle that health depends on a balance of elements
    whose result is *harmonia*: see Huffmann 1993, 45f. Cf. also Aristotle, *On
    Soul* 4.407b30–2, transl. Huffman 1993, where we are told that,
    according to some philosophers, 'soul is a kind of *harmonia*. Indeed (sc.
    they say) also that *harmonia* is a blending and combination of opposites
    and *the body is composed of opposites*' (italics mine).

66 See especially Plato, *Phaedo* 36.86c–d, transl. North Fowler 1914: 'Now
    if the soul is a harmony, it is clear that when the body is too much
    relaxed or is too tightly strung by diseases or other ills, the soul must of
    necessity perish, no matter how divine it is, like other harmonies in
    sounds and in all the works of artists, and the remains of each body will
    endure a long time until they are burnt or decayed. Now what shall we
    say *to this argument, if anyone claims that the soul, being a mixture of the
    elements of the body*, is the first to perish in what is called death?' (italics
    mine). Cf. Aristotle, *Politics* 8.1340b17–19: 'There also seems to be a
    close relation of some sort between the soul and *harmoniai* and
    rhythms, which is why many wise men say either that the soul is a
    harmonia, or that it contains one'. See also Macrobius, *Commentary on
    the Dream of Scipio* 1.14.19 (fifth century CE): 'Pythagoras and Philolaus
    said that the soul was *harmonia*' (for the suggestion that this passage of
    Macrobius is actually based on an overreading of Plato's discussion in
    the *Phaedo*, see Huffmann 1993, 327; cf. Huffmann 2009 and Trabattoni
    2023, 107).

67 Cf. Plato, *Republic* 4.443d–e, transl. Emlyn-Jones and Preddy 2013: 'A
    man does not allow the individual faculties within him to get involved in

the functions of others, nor the parts of the soul to meddle with each other, but he puts what are really his own interests in good order, directs and disciplines himself, becomes a friend to himself and *arranges those three elements together like, simply, the three defining notes of the scale, lower, upper and middle,* and any others that happen to lie in between. *He binds these all together and from many elements becomes in every respect a unity, temperate and harmonious*' (italics mine). For the *Phaedo,* see n. 66.

Chapter 2

1 Because the essential ingredients of Greek music were words, melody and rhythm (Plato, *Republic* 3.398d, cf. III.3), the three main varieties of science concerned with music were metrics, harmonics and rhythmics.

2 Before being formalized in written texts, ideas on musical issues were, for a long time, elaborated and disseminated through public speeches in front of an audience, as Plato clearly implies in some passages of the *Republic,* in Books 3 (400d4ff.) and 7 (531b2ff., cf. I.1).

3 Aristotle is also the first author to use the word *harmonikē* (sc. *epistēmē*). In *Republic* 7.531b8, Plato calls the discipline *epistēmē peri harmonias* (lit. 'science on *harmonia*') while, in *Phaedrus* 268e6, the topic is labelled *ta harmonika* (lit. 'harmonic matters').

4 Concurrently, when parts of the Greek-speaking East succumbed to the Muslim conquest, many Greek pedagogical texts were translated into Arabic, where they contributed much to the development of Arab music theory (Shiloah 1979–2003).

5 Despite what Boethius says at the beginning of his *Fundamentals of Music* 1.2 ('Thus, at the outset, it seems proper to tell someone examining music what we shall discover *about the number of kinds of music recognised by those schooled in it',* transl. Bower 989, italics mine), the tripartition appears to us as a novelty. It was probably borrowed from the threefold philosophical division of science into theoretical, productive and practical (which originated with Aristotle) and was adapted to the musical realm (Restani 2019a; Panti 2020). For the importance of Boethius as philosopher, see Marenbon 2021.

6 The most important among these medieval theoretical writings are: the treatise *De harmonica institutione* attributed to Hucbald of St Amand (*c.* 850–930), where the Boethian double octave scale system is for the first time adopted as a descriptive basis for the modal theory; the work called *Alia musica* (consisting of at least three layers, all anonymous, see Chailley 1965; *contra* Atkinson 2009), where the seven species of the octave are openly integrated with the eight church modes (Powers and Wiering 2001). On the idea, sometimes mentioned in late antiquity, that the *Oktōēchos* (i.e. the eight-mode system used in Byzantine religious chant) was also based on the ancient Greek modal system, see now Wolfram 2021.

7 Vincenzo Galilei was unable to read Greek, so he relied on the authority of Mei: Palisca 1985, 265ff.

8 In his *Discorso sopra la musica antica et moderna* (Venice 1602, esp. 8f.), Girolamo Mei condemns the prevailing contrapuntal style – in which the intertwining of different melodic lines puts the poetic text in the background – in favour of the monody used by the ancient Greeks, the only one capable (in his opinion) of moving the feelings.

9 In the preface to his *Euridice* (1601), which is the earliest surviving opera, the Italian composer Jacopo Peri (1561–1633) underlines the (ideal) continuity between ancient tragedy and opera in representing on stage characters who spoke by singing. On the real forerunners of melodrama, see Pirrotta and Povoledo 1982.

10 This same example was later re-edited by other French theorists, as Pierre Maillart (*Les tons ou discours sur les modes*, Tournay 1610, 131) and Solomon de Caus (*Institution Harmonique*, Francfort 1615, 2).

11 Summaries of the debate on the authenticity of this fragment may be found in Mountford 1936 and Pöhlmann 1970.

12 Alypius (fourth–fifth century CE) was author of the most complete and exhaustive ancient treatise discussing Greek musical notation, titled *Musical Introduction* and among the works published by Meibom. According to some anecdotal sources (discussed in Lundberg 2023, 35ff.), Meibom went beyond pure theoretical interests in ancient Greek music, as he also attempted vocal performances and reconstructions of ancient instruments.

13 This work later merged into the *Compendium of the Treatise on the Genres and Modes of Music* (Rome 1635), in which Doni tried to stimulate the application of the ancient precepts to modern musical composition. He also wrote *On the Superiority of Ancient Music* (Florence 1647), a dialogue among four characters on the merits of ancient vs modern music (IV.1).

14 This is just the most famous of the various experimental instruments invented by Doni, as the 'diharmonic' and 'triharmonic' harpsichords or the Barberini harp (Palisca and Barbieri 2001; Granata and Waanders 2015). Doni dedicated an entire essay to the description of the *lyra Barberina*, written between 1632 and 1635 but published only more than a century later (Florence 1763).

15 As stated in his *Ancient Music Adapted to Modern Practice* (Rome 1555) and other theoretical writings. On his insistence on Greek chromatic and enharmonic genres, see Kaufmann 1963; more in general on Vicentino as theoretician, see Cattin 1976; Kaufmann and Kendrick 2001.

16 On the history and great influence of Pythagoreanism throughout history, with more than one contribution on music, see, e.g., Huffmann 2014; Renger and Stavru 2016.

17 Pythagoreans shared the thesis that the sound is caused by an impact of objects with other Presocratic philosophers, such as Empedocles of Acragas and Democritus of Abdera (quoted by Theophratus, *On Senses* 9.39–41, 55–7). In fr. 1 DK, Archytas also examines the difference between high-pitched and low-pitched sounds, attributing such a difference to the speed and the strength of their movement.

18 Nine is the arithmetic mean between 12 and 6, 8 is the harmonic mean between 12 and 6; observe that the ratios 12:9 and 9:8 are equivalent to 4:3, representing the fourth, and that 12:8 and 9:6 are equivalent to 3:2, representing the fifth. The insertion of the arithmetic and harmonic means was also fundamental to the process by which the World Soul is built in Plato's *Timaeus* 35a1–36b6 (cf. n. 33).

19 The story probably originated with Nicomachus in the second century CE (see ch. 6 of his *Manual of Harmonics*, 245.19–248.26) and it was later retold, with some differences, by many authors, including Boethius (*Fundamentals of Music* 1.1).

20 In his *Discourses and Mathematical Demonstrations Regarding Two New Sciences* (Leiden 1638, Day one, 100), Galileo demonstrates that, for determining its pitch, not only the length of a string, but also its tension and weight (to which other ratios need to be applied to get a correct result) are important.

21 This proof was faithfully interpreted for the first time in Western history by Giovanni Maria Artusi (*c.* 1540–1613) in *L'Artusi, overo Delle imperfettioni della moderna musica ragionamenti dui,* Venice 1600, fols 31v–32v.

22 Leon Battista Alberti, *De pictura*, written between 1435 and 1436 but published in Basilea only in 1540 (cf. IV.4); Jacopo Barozzi da Vignola, *Regola delli cinque ordini d'architettura*, Roma 1562. On the role of mathematical model in the speculative and practical thought about music in the Renaissance, see Vendrix 2008.

23 In order to accept number 8, Zarlino describes the minor sixth as made up of the fourth (8:6) and the minor third (6:5), whose harmonic mean is 6 (Part 1, ch. 16: 'tai termini sono capaci d'un mezano termine harmonico, ch'è il 6').

24 This tuning had been rediscovered by the Italian music theorist and composer Franchinus Gaffurius (1451–1522) who, some years before Zarlino, described it in his *De harmonia musicorum instrumentorum opus* (*Work on the Harmony of Musical Instruments*), Milan 1518.

25 The application of Zarlino's criteria for consonances worked better in the vocal medium thanks to the singers' capacity to adopt a flexible intonation, while it was more complicated on instruments, as he himself acknowledged (cf., e.g., *Le istitutioni armoniche* 3.45, where he says that the singers should tune their voices *trying to adjust them to consonance*, lit. 'cercando di accomodarle alla consonanza').

26 See also Nolan 2002, 289ff., pointing out the twentieth-century intensification of the bond between music theory and new branches of mathematics as, e.g., in set theory and group theory (on which see Nolan 2010, 289–95).

27 In Grisey's theory of temporality, time is treated as a constituent element of sound itself: for an in-depth analysis of *Le Noir de l'Étoile*

and its importance for understanding Grisey's concept of musical time, see Exarchos 2018.

28 The *intermedi* were very popular entertainments in the Renaissance and Baroque periods: they involved singing, acting and dancing and were usually performed between the acts of a spoken play, in this occasion a comedy by the Italian poet, lawyer and writer Girolamo Bargagli (1537–86) titled *The Pilgrim Woman* (cf. Walker 1963; Marignetti 1996; Ketterer 1999).

29 These are the words of the official report of the event. The representation was a clear reference to Plato, *Republic* 10.617b–c, where Plato describes the experience of Er in the underworld and his vision of the universe, as also de' Rossi openly explains (*Description of the apparatus and the 'intermedi'* [. . .] 18).

30 Aristotle, *On the Heavens* 2.9.291a8 (cf. *Metaphysics* 1.5.986a2f.); Ps.-Plutarch, *On Music* 44.1147a; Porphyry, *The Life of Pythagoras* 30; Iamblichus, *On the Pythagorean Way of Life* 65; Censorinus, *The Birthday Book* 13.

31 The two works are strictly connected, since it is explicitly said that the events of the *Timaeus* take place the day after Socrates described the ideal State (which took place in the *Republic*).

32 A similar meaning of *harmonia* is also in Philolaus fr. 6a DK (cf. I.4). In *Republic* 7.530c–531c, while discussing the intellectual education of philosopher-rulers, Plato describes music (i.e. harmonic science) as a pure theoretical discipline, whose task should be the revelation of truths transcending the sphere of acoustic perception, i.e. the search for 'which numbers are concordant and which are not, and why each are so' (531c, transl. Barker 1989). These observations anticipate the description of musical *harmonia* in Book 10 of the *Republic*.

33 The process of creation has three stages. First stage: the craftsman divides the mixed substance in lengths based on two geometric progressions in which each number doubles or triples the former (here multiplied by 6 in order to obtain whole numbers in the later stage of the process: 6, 12, 24, 48 and 6, 18, 54, 162). Second stage: these double and triple ratios are filled in with harmonic and arithmetic means (in bold: 6, **8, 9,** 12, **16, 18,** 24, **32, 36,** 48 and 6, **9, 12,** 18, **27, 36,** 54, **81, 108,**

162) in order to obtain ratios corresponding to the intervals in a
Pythagorean scale: octaves (108:54, 48:24, 24:12, 12:6 = 2:1), fifths
(162:108, 81:54, 12:8, 9:6 = 3:2), fourths (108:81, 16:12, 12:9, 8:6 = 4:3)
and intervals of a tone (54:48, 27:24 = 9:8). Third stage: the fourths are
finally turned into diatonic tetrachords when all the epitritics (i.e. the
fourths, in the ratio 4:3) are filled up 'with the epogdoic kind of interval
(i.e. the tone, in the ratio 9:8), leaving a part of each of them, where the
interval of the remaining part had as its boundaries, number to number,
256 to 243' (i.e. the smaller Pythagorean semitone described by
Philolaus in fr. 6a DK, later known as the *leimma*: transl. Barker 2007).

34 Many of these commentaries were specifically devoted to its musical
parts, like *On the Generation of the Soul in the Timaeus* by Plutarch of
Chaeronea (*c.* 46–119 CE). The *Timaeus* had a wide diffusion in late
antiquity, becoming the only Platonic text known to the Latin West
during the early Middle Ages (although not completely, since both
Cicero, 106–43 BCE, and Calcidius, fourth century CE, omitted parts of
the original text in their translations: on Calcidius and cosmic harmony,
see Hoenig 2020).

35 This idea appears at the very beginning of Boethius' text, see
Fundamentals of Music 1.1, transl. Bower 1989: 'What Plato rightfully
said can likewise be understood: the soul of the universe was joined
together according to musical concord'.

36 In order to leave his Aristotelianism intact, Pirrotta (1968, 254f.) limits
Dante's reference to a cosmic music, perceptible with the senses, to
these verses of the *Paradise*, which describe the poet and Beatrice
passing through the realm of fire *before* entering the first sphere.

37 Among those who believed in a sonorous universe we may quote:
Cicero, *Dream of Scipio* 5.18f.; Pliny, *Natural History* 2.20; Nicomachus,
Manual of Harmonics ch. 3; Theon of Smyrna, *Mathematics Useful for
Understanding Plato* 140–7; Ptolemy, *Harmonics* 3.8–16; Macrobius,
Commentary on the Dream of Scipio 2.2.19; Boethius, *Fundamentals of
Music* 1.27.

38 On the inaudibility of planetary music see, e.g., Proclus, *Commentary on
Plato's Republic* 2.242.29–243.3 (who, however, recognized that this
intellectual activity can also have a sensible expression) and Simplicius,

Commentary on Aristotle's On the Heavens 2.9, 469.18–20: on both these authors cf. Pelosi 2018, 23ff. The same idea is alluded to in *Psalm* 19.4 (talking about the heavens announcing the glory of God: Haupt 1919): 'There is no speech or words, their voice is inaudible'. On the role played by cosmic harmony in Middle Platonism, see Petrucci 2020.

39 Ficino's annotated translation of the *Timaeus* (published in his 1484 *Platonis Opera Omnia*) was the first complete Latin translation of this text (cf. n. 34 above) and made this important source on divine harmony accessible to a wider audience of readers (Allen 2003).

40 Cf. Plutarch, *Table-Talk* 8.2.718c, transl. Minar 1961: 'If you please, let us on Plato's birthday take Plato himself as partner in the conversation, and since we have spoken about the gods, consider what he had in mind when *he asserted that God is always doing geometry* – if indeed this statement is to be attributed to Plato' (italics mine).

41 For the announcement, see https://www.youtube.com/watch?v=aEPIwE JmZyE.

42 Robert Fludd was harshly attacked by Kepler for basing his harmonies on abstract numbers and for presupposing the centrality of the Earth (Field 1984; Gozza 2000, 49).

43 Cf. *Exhortation to the Greeks* 1.5.2–3, transl. Butterworth 1919: 'this pure song [. . .] reduced this whole to harmony [. . .] On this many-voiced instrument of the universe He makes music to God'.

44 *Exhortation to the Greeks* 1.5.3, transl. Butterworth 1919: 'By the power of the Holy Spirit He arranged in harmonious order this great world, yes, and the little world of man too, body and soul together'.

45 For a new edition comparing all the manuscript evidence transmitting this text, see now Macaskill 2013.

46 Time is a central topic in Augustine's thought: see especially *Confessions* 11.17–41.

Chapter 3

1 According to Starr (2013), the aesthetic experience emerges from interactions, among different areas of the brain, which are valid across

all the arts and therefore produce the same emotions, despite addressing different senses. For a general survey on the phenomenon of *cultural turns*, see Bachmann-Medick 2016 [2006].

2   See Homer, *Iliad* 18.70–2 (transl. Murray, rev. by Wyatt 1925), where Achilles laments the death of Patroclus while his mother Thetis tries to rescue him from his grief: 'Then to his side, as he groaned heavily (*bary stenachōn*), came his queenly mother, and with a shrill cry (*oxy de kōkysasa*) she clasped the head of her son, and with wailing spoke to him winged words' (*epea pteroenta*, i.e. 'words that fly' straight to the target, as if they were winged arrows: Durante 1958, Letoublon 1999).

3   The third qualification, in which Plato recognizes the real expertise of the judges, involves attributes of an ethical kind. On this passage, see Rocconi 2012 and Barker 2013.

4   The context described in this dialogue is quite different from that of *Republic* Book 7 (cf. I.1) and *Timaeus* 35a–36d (cf. II.3), which focus on the intelligible realm instead.

5   See Plato, *Laws* 2.654a (quoted also in ch. I.2): 'these same gods have given the capacity to perceive rhythm and *harmonia*, and to enjoy them (*meth' hēdonēs*)'. Cf. *Laws* 2.663b: 'the teaching which refuses to separate the pleasant (*hēdy*) from the just helps'.

6   Aristoxenus, *Elements* of *Harmonics* 8.23 and *passim*. According to Aristotle (*On the Soul* 427b14–16), *phantasia* gives rise to sensorial after-images (*phantasmata*) which, once memorized, enable us to summarize what we perceive at the present moment and what we have perceived in the past. On the importance of sense-perception for the conceptual representation of reality in Aristotelian thought, see Tovanen 2022.

7   On the importance of acoustic perception for evaluation purposes, cf. *Elements of Harmonics* 14.14–15, transl. Barker 1989: '[...] two things, that which utters sound and *that which discriminates it* (*to krinon*), these being the voice and the hearing (*akoē*)' (italics mine).

8   Aristoxenus, *Elements of Harmonics* 38.31f., transl. Barker 1989: 'It is in a process of coming to be (*en genesei*) that melody consists, as do all the other parts of music' (cf. 33.29–32: 'Further, we must not forget that musical understanding involves the simultaneous grasp of one thing that remains constant and another that changes').

9   The most important information on Aristoxenus' concerns on musical judgment may be read in Ps.-Plutarch, *On Music* chapters 34–36 (1143e–1144e), quoting and paraphrasing genuine Aristoxenian material: on these pieces of evidence, see Barker 2007, 236–59.

10 Cf. the use of the same verb in Cleonides, *Harmonic Introduction* ch. 13, 206.6f., summarizing lost Aristoxenian material on harmonics.

11 Neither here nor anywhere else does Aristoxenus mention the idea that music is imitative.

12 Cf. Ps.-Plutarch, *On Music* 33.1143a–b, transl. Barker 1984: 'our view is that the cause of *ēthos* is a particular kind of combination (*synthesis*) or mixture (*mixis*) or both'. The components of this mixture (melody, rhythm and text) are exemplified shortly after, cf. 35.1144a: 'Three minimal items must always fall on the hearing simultaneously, the note, the duration, and the syllable or letter'.

13 See Ps.-Plutarch, *On Music* 36.1144c–d, transl. Barker 1984: 'One cannot become a complete musician and critic just on the basis of what we treat as the department of music as a whole [. . .] One cannot become a good critic on the basis of these (sc. technical elements) alone'.

14 Elsewhere in Aristoxenus' *Elements of Harmonics* (23.6), enharmonic melodies are described as 'the most beautiful' (*kallistē*) kind of music.

15 In a fragment of the fourth-century BCE philosopher Speusippus of Athens (fr. 75, on which Tarán 1981, 431–5; Barker 2012, 308ff.), head of the Academy on Plato's death in 348/347 BCE, we may read a similar description of a not innate (*autophyēs*) kind of perception which is typical of the *mousikos* who 'grasps both what is attuned and what is not attuned' (he calls it 'knowing' or 'cognitive perception'/*epistēmonikē aisthēsis*, for the same expression, see also Diogenes of Babylon, quoted above; on the possibility that this expression is not by Speusippus, see Tarán 1981, 432f.).

16 See especially the seminal work of the American psychologist Jerome Bruner (1915–2016), from Bruner and Brown 1956 onwards.

17 Since Ekman 1971, this has become a dominant position within psychological studies. For a discussion and reassessment of the influence of neo-Darwinian positions on the Humanities, see Gross 2006 and 2010.

18 On the topic of emotions in Aristotle, see especially Fortenbaugh 2002
    [1975]; Konstan 2006.
19 Cf. Ps.-Aristotle, *Problems* 19.38, transl. Barker 1984: 'Why does
    everyone enjoy rhythm and melody and the whole class of concords? Is
    it because we naturally enjoy all natural movements? An indication of
    this is that children enjoy these things from the moment they are born'.
20 The story is told also in Philodemus, *On Music* 4, col. 42.39–45 Delattre;
    Sextus Empiricus, *Against the Mathematicians* 6.8; Cicero, *On His
    Policies* fr. 2 [4.992] *apud* Boethius, *Fundamentals of Music* 1.1;
    Quintilian, *The Orator's Education* 1.10.32. On ethnic modes, see II.1
    and IV.3. On the *spondeion*, a libation tune attributed to the mythical
    Phrygian aulete Olympus, see Barker 2011.
21 The seventeenth- and eighteenth-century theorists René Descartes
    (*Compendium musicae*, 1618), Athanasius Kircher (*Musurgia
    universalis*, 1650: Books 7 to 9) and Johann Mattheson (*Der
    vollkommene Capellmeister*, 1739) argued that musical composers could
    express specific affects in their music by using specific parameters (e.g.
    duration and pitch, according to Descartes, who later in his life will
    dedicate an important work to the topic of the emotions, *Les Passions de
    l'âme*, 1649) or corresponding musical figures (especially melodic
    intervals, whose affective properties were of interest to Mattheson). For
    a summary of this cultural phenomenon, see Buelow 2001.
22 Contagion and empathy are listed as 'route D' and 'route E' in the
    'Component Process Model of emotion' (CPM) developed by the
    psychologist Klaus Scherer and his team to identify the major and
    interrelated factors responsible for emotion induction (Scherer 2009;
    Scherer and Coutinho 2013, 138f.). On the difference between these two
    processes, cf. also Coplan 2006, 32: 'In a sense, emotional contagion
    responses are more physiological than empathy responses. Contagion
    responses rely on direct sensory stimulation and subsequent
    physiological responses to that stimulation. Empathy responses, on the
    other hand, necessarily involve affect but also involve higher order
    cognition and the imagination'. On musical expressiveness, see
    especially Section 1 of the collection of essays edited by Cochrane,
    Fantini and Scherer 2013.

23 The term 'empathy' (whose fundamentals may be traced back to the German philosopher and psychologist Theodor Lipps (1851–1914) and his theory of *Einfühlung*, lit. 'feeling into') was introduced into the English language in 1909 by the psychologist Edward Titchener (1867–1927). Before him, the term commonly used to refer to empathy-related phenomena was 'sympathy'. On the topic, see, e.g., Stueber 2019; Lanzoni 2018.

24 On the mechanism of *sympatheia*, see also *Problems* 7.5, transl. Mayhew 2011 (the whole book is titled *Problems arising from Sympathy*): 'Why do some things painful to hear make us shudder – for instance, sharpening a saw, cutting a pumice stone, and grinding a stone – but the visual signs of their effects (*sēmeia tōn pathōn*) (on others) produce those very effects (*pathē*) in us?' It is interesting to notice that, also according to modern neuroscience, empathy and imitation are intimately connected. They can be viewed as means to experiencing and understanding mental and affective states of oneself and others (Decety and Meltzoff 2011).

25 On the music-to-listener emotional contagion, see especially Davies 2011 (ch. 4) and 2013; cf. Juslin 2019 (ch. 20). Emotional contagion is widely recognized by modern scholars as one of the mechanisms by which an emotional response to music might be induced (Juslin and Västfjäll 2008).

26 In the eighteenth century, the Swiss-born philosopher Jean-Jacques Rousseau (1712–78) gives a similar priority to melody over harmony, emphasizing the ability of melody alone to *imitate* and thus move the passions: see the entry 'Melody' in his *Dictionary of Music* (Paris 1768), on which cf. Cohen 2013.

27 In approximately the same period, similar topics are discussed by another Peripatetic philosopher. In a passage of the *Elements of Harmonics* (48.13f.), Aristoxenus explicitly describes musical melody as a process of 'coming to be' (*genesis*). This is why, for him, memory (*mnēmē*) has such an outstanding role in our understanding of music, cf. 48.14–18, transl. Barker 1989: 'comprehension of music comes from two things, perception and memory: for we have to perceive what is coming to be and remember what has come to be. There is no other way of following the contents of music'.

28 Cf. Aristides Quintilianus, *On Music* 1.15, transl. Barker 1989: 'the sound runs quickly across the short syllables and pauses when it comes to the long one'.

29 The mimetic character of instrumental music is exemplified by the evidence on the auletic melody called *Pythikos nomos* (on *nomos*, see IV.1), described as a representation (*dēlōma*) of the battle of Apollo against the snake Pytho (Pollux, *Onomasticon* 4.84; Strabo, *Geography* 9.3.10). In this kind of composition, the musicians imitated the various phases of the battle, including the sounds of gnashing teeth and hissing serpent on the pipes, with special sound effects realized on the aulos (Rocconi 2014).

30 On the meaning of *phantasia* in Aristotle, see above, esp. n. 6.

31 Cf., e.g., *On Music* 2.14, 80.10–22. The page number of Aristides Quintilianus' text refers to the Teubner edition of the treatise (Winnington-Ingram 1963).

32 According to Ptolemy, *Harmonics* 3.5, 96.24, transl. Barker 1989, *ennoia* is 'concerned with the retention and memory of the stamped impressions'.

33 On the aesthetics of David Hume, see especially Gracyk 2021.

34 The first text in which we find a possible – although not so clear – explanation of the special status of the ratios expressing concords is *The Division of the Canon* attributed to Euclid (*c.* 300 BCE). In this text we are told that concords need to be expressed by multiple (mn/n) or epimoric ratios (n+1/n), because the terms of their ratios are numbers 'spoken of in relation to one another by a single name' (149.11–14). Cf. Ps.-Aristotle, *Problems* 19.41, transl. Barker 1989: 'concord exists between notes that are well-rationed to one another' (on the interpretation of this statement, possibly pre-dating the *Division*, see Barker 2007, 375f.).

35 In Plato's *Timaeus* (80b, transl. Barker 1989, cf. II.3), the mathematical excellence of music is *mimesis* of the divine: musical concords give pleasure (*hēdonē*) or a higher kind of delight (*euphrosynē*) 'because of the imitation (*mimesis*) of the divine *harmonia* that comes into being in mortal movements'.

36 The four 'parts' (*merē*) of the octave-*harmonia* are its boundaries or fixed notes delimiting tetrachords, namely *nētē, paramesē, mesē, hypatē*; the 'magnitudes' (*megethē*) are the ratios expressing the most important

intervals, the octave, the fifth and the fourth (12:9 and 8:6, which are 'equal in measure' since each is equivalent to 4:3; 12:8 and 9:6, equivalent to 3:2); finally, the 'excesses' (*hyperochai*) are the arithmetical differences between the ratios' terms. While the excesses in the ratios between the extremes and their harmonic mean are, in a related sense, equal in measure (since the difference between 12 and 8 is one third of 12 and that between 8 and 6 is one third of 6), the excesses in the ratios between the extremes and their arithmetic mean are equal in number (12-6 and 9-6 = 3). On this fragment, see especially Barker 2007, 329–38; cf. Rocconi 2011.

37 Aristoxenus establishes frequent parallels between the combination of notes in melody and the combination of letters in language, both governed by similar rules of internal coherence. See, e.g., *Elements of Harmonics* 37.2–6, transl. Barker 1989: 'And yet the order which relates to the melodic and unmelodic is similar to that concerned with the combination of letters in speech: from a given set of letters a syllable is not generated in just any way, but in some ways and not in others'.

38 We have evidence on the existence of a famous book titled *The Canon*, written by the fifth-century BCE artist Polyclitus, which since antiquity have had an outstanding influence on Western sculpture and theory of art. In this (now lost) treatise – we are told by Galen, *On the Doctrines of Hippocrates and Plato* 16 – Polyclitus gave rigid instructions on the desirable *symmetriae* of the human body, namely on the size of the various parts of the body to one another, also supporting his ideas with the statue of a man realized according to the tenets of his treatise. The same authority is quoted by Lucian of Samosata (*c.* 120–200 CE) in his dialogue *On Dancing* 75, when talking about the desirable body proportions of the pantomimic dancer.

39 Cf. Ptolemy, *Harmonics* 1.7, transl. Barker 1989: 'How the ratios of the concords may be correctly defined'.

Chapter 4

1 In some Christian authors, for instance (as Clement of Alexandria (*c.* 150–211 CE), quoted at II.4), the difference between pagan and

Christian music is outlined in terms of *old* versus *new* (Kramarz 2018 sees here a direct echo of the New Music criticism described below). For a similar opposition *ancient* vs *modern* in the culture of early China, cf. DeWoskin 1982, esp. ch. 6 (I thank Irene Crosignani for bringing this parallel to my attention).

2   The expression *Ars Nova* was used as a historical slogan by the German musicologist Johannes Wolf (1869–1947) in his *Geschichte der Mensural-Notation von 1250–1460* (Leipzig 1904) and became a common label in subsequent scholarship. However, it was also the title of a treatise written, about 1322, by the French theorist and composer Philippe de Vitry (1291–1361).

3   The controversy between the so-called *prima* and *seconda pratica* (lit. 'first and second practice') publicly arose when the theorist Giovanni Maria Artusi (*c.* 1540–1613), in his *On the Imperfections of Modern Music* (Venice 1600), attacked the composer Claudio Monteverdi (1567–1643) for his unconventional treatment of dissonance. The latter, following Plato's *Republic* 3.398d (as we are told by his brother Giulio Cesare in the explanation, published in 1607, that was meant to support Claudio's revolutionary aesthetic choices), believed that, in a song, sound and rhythm should follow the text. On this topic, see Palisca 2001b; Cohen 2022.

4   In a similar vein, in his *On the Excellence of Ancient Music* (Florence 1647) Giovanni Battista Doni uses the term *hodierna* in opposition to *antiqua* (e.g. 24, 89 and *passim*). On Doni, see also II.1.

5   In many composers, however, the fascination with antiquity continued to exert a strong influence (see Introduction).

6   On this topic, see the discussions, focusing in particular on Aristotle's *Poetics*, in Montanari 2017, 153–69, and Halliwell 2017, esp. 206 ('the schema itself – sc. of analysis of literary genres in the *Poetics* – as a fusion of genealogy and evaluation […] can be seen as a major ancestor, partly via other Peripatetic intermediaries, of what becomes a cardinal organising principle of many modern literary histories explicitly so-called'). More specifically on *mousikē*, see Tocco 2019; cf. Hadjimichael 2019.

7   With this term, scholars – following the division introduced by the Alexandrian grammarians – refer to the first period of ancient Greek

comedy, which more or less corresponds to the activity of Aristophanes of Athens.

8   The word *nun* is a modern supplement to bring out the contrast with *archaion* in line 2: other editors suggest *kainēn* (lit. 'new', sc. *mousikēn*).

9   The reference to the city of Sidon is due to the fact that Phrynichus had written a play titled *Phoenician Women* where, according to the scholia (i.e. comments inserted in the margin of the manuscript), Sidon was mentioned.

10 Actually, we do not know whether the compiler read their original writings or, rather, relied on the reports provided by Hellenistic compilers: for a discussion on this topic, see Barker 2014, chs 1–4.

11 The expression *archaia mousikē* occurs in chs 3.1131f; 4.1132e; 12.1135d; 37.1144e; 40.1145f. *Hoi palaioi* are mentioned in chs 15.1136b; 18.1137a–b; 21.1138b; 26.1140b; 34.1143e; 37.1144e. *Ta tote* vs *ta nun* in chs 15.1136b; 20.1137f; 21.1138a–b; 38.1145a.

12 By providing literary and musical criticism with *legalistic* terminology, Plato validates his interpretation of musical phenomena (which, in antiquity, were large-scale public performances provided by the city) as the trigger for social and political change. See also Plato, *Republic* 4.424c (transl. Emlyn-Jones and Freddy 2013): 'For *the forms of music are nowhere altered without affecting the greatest political laws*, as Damon in fact says, and I believe him' (italics mine).

13 According to Barker (2014, 31), some possible ways of supplementing Heraclides' title are 'Collection of *people who were eminent* in music' or 'Collection of *discoveries* in music'.

14 The term 'canon' was first introduced with this meaning by the classical scholar David Ruhnken (1723–98) in his *Critical History of Greek Orators*, published as an appendix to his 1768 book on the figures of speech of the Roman rhetorician Publius Rutilius Lupus (first century CE).

15 See, e.g., Adorno's severe criticism of jazz in his famous 1941 essay titled *On Popular Music*.

16 For the possible meanings of (and differences between) the categories of *popular* and *folk music*, see Pegg 2001; Hamm et al. 2014. It is important to point out that, from a strictly musicological perspective, it is perhaps the *folk* label (which refers more directly to the concepts of

tradition, oral transmission and *anonymity*, and is studied by ethnomusicology) that is more pertinent when, with reference to classical antiquity, we are talking about poetry and music related to non-institutional contexts and belonging to a submerged literature that has not passed the scrutiny of an official canonization (cf. n. 17). The term popular, however, is most widely used by scholars in Classical Studies.

17 A recent survey on *popular culture* in classical antiquity, with an excellent theoretical introduction, is Grig 2017. More specifically on popular literature and music, see, e.g., Yatromanolakis 2009; Neri 2021; Rocconi 2021. On the notion of *submerged* literature cf. Rossi 2000; Colesanti and Giordano 2014 (see Introduction, 1: '*submerged* literature serves as a label encompassing mainly those texts that were not protected during their transmission by social contexts and institutions and were therefore excluded by the circuits of transmission, but that can nonetheless be reconstructed'); Colesanti and Lulli 2016; Ercolani and Giordano 2016.

18 For other nuances of meaning suggested by this term, see Karin Schlapbach's remarks at https://research-bulletin.chs.harvard. edu/2011/02/12/what-exactly-is-pandemos-mousike/.

19 Alexandrian poets conventionally used ancient lyric verses (i.e. verses originally sung to the accompaniment of a musical instrument) in repeated stichic patterns (i.e. verses of the same kind repeated in every line of the text).

20 On the role attributed here to the 'Muse of Euripides' (probably realized by a potsherds player through which 'the poet would have poked fun at the Euripidean erotic-and-exotic inspiration'), see De Simone 2008, 489.

21 The comedy is set in the underworld, since in 405 BCE both the dramatists were actually dead.

22 The opposition aulos vs lyre (a cliché in this particular historical period) here seems to convey an opposition between *vulgar* musical genres, on the one hand, and *dignified* ones, on the other. The sentence 'who needs a lyre for (Euripides') job?' seems in fact a precise reference to Aeschylus's use of the string instrument in the previous lines (1281–97), where there was a clear reference to the great citharodic tradition of which the poet had proclaimed himself heir.

23 The rescue operation is divided into two steps (the first at 459-72 ~ 486-99; the second at 512-19), which employ two different rhythmic patterns in order to characterize the two moments of the collective action: the anapaestic rhythm (U U —) is used when the statue is still at the bottom of the cave and the movements are necessarily more widely spaced and slower, while the swifter iambic rhythm (U —) is performed when the effort is coming to an end and the gestures are, consequently, denser and faster. On this passage and its resemblance with work songs with a similar function and structure in different ethnographic contexts (e.g. the tuna butchers' songs still performed in South Italy), see Rocconi 2016b.

24 A similar allusion to forms of popular music may be found in the monody of Ion in the Euripidean tragedy of that name (*Ion* 83-143), the so-called *hymn to the broom*, the Apollonian prayer that Ion sings at the beginning of the drama as he sweeps the steps of the temple with a broom of laurel. On these and other Euripidean scenes alluding to the wide and varied category of the *popular*, see Rocconi 2016b and 2021.

25 Bakhtin 1981. Yatromanolakis (2009, 263 and *passim*, cf. Yatromanolakis and Roilos 2003, 51) uses the word 'interdiscursivity'.

26 The peculiar distinction, recurring in Books 2–3 of Aristides Quintilianus' *On Music*, which classifies every element of *mousikē* (sounds, rhythms, instruments, etc.) under the category of male and female, finds no parallels in ancient theoretical sources.

27 Starting with Plato who, in the *Protagoras* 347b-c, blames the symposia of common and vulgar men who entertain themselves with *aulētrides* and, in the *Symposium* 176a, proposes to send them away from the event.

28 Most fragments are quoted in Athenaeus of Naucratis (second–third century CE), *Sophists at Dinner* Book 13, all devoted to the subject of the Greek *hetairai* (McClure 2003).

29 In recent years, the oppositional theme of *Greek* vs *Barbarian* has become a principal subject in classical scholarship: see, e.g., Hall 1989, exploring the Hellenic construction of the *barbarian* East through the lens of Attic tragedy; Gruen 2011; Vlassopoulos 2013; Rocconi 2019b.

30 According to Plato and many other fifth–fourth-century sources, the only true Greek *harmonia* is the Dorian (Plato, *Laches* 188d). It

exhibits – we are told by his pupil Heraclides of Pontus, fr. 114, transl. Schütrumpf et al. 2008 – 'manliness (*to andrōdes*) and magnificence (*to megaloprepes*), and this is not relaxed or merry, but sullen and intense, and neither varied nor complex' (in Greek perception, all of these being distinctive features of oriental music). In a fragment of the fifth-century dithyrambic poet Telestes of Selinus, the Lydian tune is said to be 'rival of the Dorian muse' (fr. 806, transl. LeVen 2010).

31 The terms 'tense' (*epiteinomenē*) and 'relaxed' (*aniemenē*, sc. *harmonia*) originally refer to the higher and lower relative pitches of these scales, due to the tension of the strings on the lyre.

32 On the significant contribution of Near-Eastern elements to the development of what we call ancient Greek music, see especially Franklin 2015 and 2020.

33 The Delian League was founded as a military alliance of Greek city-states, under the leadership of Athens, with the purpose of fighting the Persian empire: but it soon became an Athenian political instrument used to exert that city's supremacy over the other members, leading to the later internal strife among Greek city-states which will culminate in the Peloponnesian War (431–404 BCE).

34 The origin of auletic music is variously attributed, depending on the case, to mythical characters such as Marsyas, Hyagnis, or Olympus: on this, see especially Griffith 2020, 389; Sarti 2020; Panegyres 2007, esp. 267–9. On the application of the label *Asiatic* to certain aspects of Greek musical culture, see, e.g., Strabo (*c.* 63 BCE–23 CE), *Geography* 10.17.

35 Since 2017, the corpus of the ethnomusicological documents collected in Greece by Baud-Bovy has been held by the Musée d'ethnographie de Genève (https://www.meg.ch/en/research-collections/fonds-samuel-baud-bovy).

36 In 1907, Favari had published a collection of Sicilian folk songs which had been highly praised by Romagnoli.

37 The *rebetika* are Greek songs associated with an urban lowbrow milieu, which merged elements of the Turkish popular music with the Greek popular song (Holst-Warhaft 2001).

38 The tetrachordal technique is already used in the ballet *Antigone*, which premiered in London in 1960 (Levidou, Romanou and Vlastos 2016,

94ff.), and in Theodorakis' composition for symphony orchestra *To Axion esti* (1960), where he set to music the verses of Nobel Prize-winning poet Odysseas Elytis (1911–96).

39 The birthplace of rhetoric as an art is traditionally considered fifth-century BCE Sicily in the persons of Corax and Tisias, both from Syracuse (the former said to have been the author of the first handbook on the topic, the latter the tutor of Gorgias of Leontini (*c.* 483–475 BCE), who introduced rhetoric in Athens), or, according to Aristotle fr. 65 Rose, of the polymath Empedocles of Acragas (492–432 BCE).

40 Cf. Plato, *Cratylus* 424b–c, *Philebus* 17c–d, *Republic* 400b–c; Aristophanes, *Clouds* 636–51. More explicitly on the melodicity of the Greek language and on the distinction between the melody of the spoken and the sung, see Aristoxenus, *The Elements of Harmonics* 3.9–16 (and *passim*): 'The voice moves in the kind of movement I have mentioned *both when we speak and when we si*ng (since *high and low are obviously present in both of these,* and movement with respect to place is that through which high and low come about, but the two movements are not of the same form' (transl. Barker 1989, italics mine).

41 This is the meaning of *mousikos* we find in Aristoxenus, *Elements of Harmonics* 2.1–6. Aristoxenus' interest in linguistic phenomena is attested by the frequent similarities between musical and linguistic elements (*stoicheia*) occurring in his works (e.g. *Elements of Harmonics* 37.2–6, quoted in III.4, n. 37) and to which also the teacher of rhetoric Dionysius of Halicarnassus (*c.* 60–7 BCE) alludes (*On the Arrangement of Words* 14.2–4).

42 Diogenes Laertius, *Lives of Eminent Philosophers* 7.43: 'Rhetoric according to them (sc. the Stoics) may be divided into invention of arguments, their expression in words, their arrangement, and delivery'. On Hellenistic rhetorical theory, see Kremmydas and Tempest 2013. Later on, Cicero will add memory, bringing the number of the canons of rhetoric to five.

43 The *kritikoi* are known to us only from Philodemus of Gadara (*c.* 110–35 BCE), who attacks them in his treatise *On Poems*, largely by way of the Stoic Crates of Mallos (mid-second century BCE), a Greek grammarian who polemically discussed their work: 'the *kritikoi* [...]

agree that the content is external to art <and is> knowable <not> by reason, but by the trained ear (*tetrimmenē akoē*)' (Philodemus, *On Poems* 5, transl. Obbink 1995). Their ideas might have influenced Cicero too, though indirectly, as recently suggested by Porter 2018.

44 In the *Orator* (57), Cicero seems to imply that the Latin accent was still a pitch accent: 'here is, moreover, even in speech, a sort of singing' (transl. Hendrickson and Hubbell 1939).

45 For the hypothesis that a growing interest in the visual aspects of the orator's delivery was stimulated by the impact of pantomime (a theatrical performance very popular during the Roman Empire, in which a single dancer acts all the characters in a story simply by using masks and body language), see Rocconi 2022b. An example of the liveliness of the debate on the taxonomy of gesture is Maricchiolo, Gnisci and Bonaiuto 2012.

46 This groundbreaking event was followed by the discovery, six years later (1421), of a complete text of Cicero's *On the Orator,* together with his previously unknown *Brutus* and *Orator.*

Bibliography

Allen, M. J. B. (2003), 'The Ficinian *Timaeus* and Renaissance Science', in G.
Reydams-Schils (ed.), *Plato's* Timaeus *as Cultural Icon*, 238–50, Notre
Dame: University of Notre Dame Press.

Ammann, P. J. (1967), 'The Musical Theory and Philosophy of Robert Fludd',
Journal of the Warburg and Courtauld Institutes, 30: 198–227.

Atkinson, Ch. M. (2009), *The Critical Nexus: Tone-System, Mode, and
Notation in Early Medieval Music*, Oxford: Oxford University Press.

Attridge, D. (2019), *The Experience of Poetry: From Homer's Listeners to
Shakespeare's Readers*, Oxford: Oxford University Press.

Bachmann-Medick, D. (2016 [2006]), *Cultural Turns: New Orientations in
the Study of Culture*, transl. by A. Blauhut, Berlin: De Gruyter (or. edn
Reinbek bei Hamburg: Rowohlt Taschenbuch).

Bakhtin, M. (1981), *The Dialogic Imagination: Four Essays*, Austin:
University of Texas Press.

Barbieri, P. (2007), 'Pietro della Valle: The *Esthèr* oratorio (1639) and Other
Experiments in the "stylus metabolicus". With New Documents on
Triharmonic Instruments', *Recercare* 19 (1/2): 73–124.

Barker, A. (1984), *Greek Musical Writings, I: The Musician and His Art*,
Cambridge: Cambridge University Press.

Barker, A. (1989), *Greek Musical Writings, II: Harmonic and Acoustic Theory*,
Cambridge: Cambridge University Press.

Barker, A. (2001), 'Diogenes of Babylon and Hellenistic Musical Theory', in
C. Auvray-Assayas and D. Delattre (eds), *Cicéron et Philodème: la
polémique en philosophie*, 353–70, Paris: Éd. Rue d'Ulm.

Barker, A. (2007), *The Science of Harmonics in Classical Greece*, Cambridge:
Cambridge University Press.

Barker, A. (2009), 'Shifting Conceptions of "Schools" of Harmonic Theory,
400 BC–200 AD', in M. C. Martinelli (ed.), *La Musa dimenticata. Aspetti
dell'esperienza musicale greca in età ellenistica*, 165–90, Pisa: Edizioni
della Normale.

Barker, A. (2010), 'Mathematical Beauty Made Audible: Musical Aesthetics in Ptolemy's *Harmonics*', *Classical Philology* 105 (4): 403–20.

Barker, A. (2011), 'The Music of Olympus', *Quaderni Urbinati di Cultura Classica* 99 (3): 43–57.

Barker, A. (2012), 'Aristoxenus and the Early Academy', in C. A. Huffmann (ed.), *Aristoxenus of Tarentum. Discussion*, 297–324, Piscataway, NJ: Transaction Publishers.

Barker, A. (2013), 'The *Laws* and Aristoxenus on the Criteria of Musical Judgement', in A.-E. Peponi (ed.), *Performance and Culture in Plato's Laws*, 392–416, Cambridge: Cambridge University Press.

Barker, A. (2014), *Ancient Greek Writers on Their Musical Past*, Pisa-Rome: Serra editore.

Barrett, L. (2011), *Beyond the Brain: How Body and Environment Shape Animal and Human Minds*, Princeton, NJ: Princeton University Press.

Barrett, L. and K. A. Lindquist (2008), 'The Embodiment of Emotion', in G. R. Semin and E. R. Smith (eds), *Embodied Grounding: Social, Cognitive, Affective, and Neuroscientific Approaches*, 237–62, Cambridge: Cambridge University Press.

Bartels, M. L. (2012), '*Senex Mensura*: An Objective Aesthetics of Seniors in Plato's *Laws*', in I. Sluiter and R. M. Rosen (eds), *Aesthetic Value in Classical Antiquity*, 133–58, Leiden-Boston: Brill.

Bartoš, H. (2015), *Philosophy and Dietetics in the Hippocratic* On Regimen*: A Delicate Balance of Health*, Leiden-Boston: Brill.

Bartusiak, M. (2000), *Einstein's Unfinished Symphony: Listening to the Sounds of Space-Time*, Washington, DC: Joseph Henry Press.

Baumbach, M. (2006), '*Protos heuretes*', in H. Cancik and H. Schneider (eds), *Brill's New Pauly*, DOI: http://dx.doi.org/10.1163/1574-9347_bnp_e1011460.

Becker, J. (1986), 'Is Western Art Music Superior?', *The Musical Quarterly* 72 (13): 341–59.

Bélis, A. (2008), 'Théodore Reinach et la musique grecque', in S. Basch, M. Espagne and J. Leclant (eds), *Les frères Reinach: colloque réuni les 22 et 23 juine 2007 2 et 23 juin 2007 à l'Académie des inscriptions et belles-lettres*, 165–76, Paris: Éditions de Boccard.

Bellia, A. (2021), 'Towards a Digital Approach to the Listening to Ancient Places', *Heritage* 4 (3): 2470–81.

Berger, P. L. and Th. Luckmann (1966), *The Social Construction of Reality: A Treatise in the Sociology of Knowledge*, New York: Anchor Books.

Bergquist, P., rev. by S. Keyl (2001), 'Tritonius, Petrus', in *Grove Music Online*, DOI: https://doi.org/10.1093/gmo/9781561592630.article.28405.

Bernhard, M. (2007), 'Il *De institutione musica* di Boezio nell'alto Medioevo', In M. Cristiani, C. Panti and P. Graziano (eds), *Harmonia mundi: Musica mondana e musica celeste fra Antichità e Medioevo*, 77–93, Florence: SISMEL-Edizioni del Galluzzo.

Besso, G., B. Guagliumi and F. Pezzoli (2008), 'La riscoperta della *Politica* di Aristotele nell'Italia di età umanistico-rinascimentale tra interpretazione filologico-letteraria e filosofico-politica', *Quaderni del Dipartimento di filologia A. Rostagni* 7: 147–64.

Bithell, C. and J. Hill, eds (2013), *The Oxford Handbook of Music Revival*, Oxford: Oxford University Press.

Blažeković, Z. (2012), 'Vesuvian Organology in Charles Burney's General History of Music', in R. Eichmann, J. Fang and L.-Ch. Kock (eds), *Sound from the Past: The Interpretation of Musical Artifacts in an Archaeological Context*, 39–57, Rahden, Westf.: Leidorf.

Bod, R., J. Maat and T. Weststeijn (2010), *The Making of the Humanities I: Early Modern Europe*, Amsterdam: Amsterdam University Press.

Bod, R., J. Maat and T. Weststeijn (2012), *The Making of the Humanities II: From Early Modern to Modern Disciplines*, Amsterdam: Amsterdam University Press.

Bod, R., J. Maat and T. Weststeijn (2014), *The Making of the Humanities III: The Modern Humanities*, Amsterdam: Amsterdam University Press.

Botstein, L. (2001), 'Modernism', in *Grove Music Online*, DOI: https://doi.org/10.1093/gmo/9781561592630.article.40625.

Bower, C. M., transl. (1989), *Anicius Manlius Severinus Boethius, Fundamentals of Music*, New Haven-London: Yale University Press.

Bregman, A. S. (1994), *Auditory Scene Analysis: The Perceptual Organization of Sound*, Cambridge, MA-London: The MIT Press.

Briggs, Ch. F. (1999), *Giles of Rome's De regimine principum*, Cambridge: Cambridge University Press.

Briggs, Ch. F. and P. Eardley, eds (2016), *A Companion to Giles of Rome*, Leiden-Boston: Brill.

Brisson, L. (2021), 'How to Make a Soul in the *Timaeus*', in Ch. Jorgenson, F. Karfík and Š. Špinka (eds), *Plato's Timaeus. Proceedings of the Tenth Symposium Platonicum Pragense*, 70–91, Leiden-Boston: Brill.

Brook, P. (1968), *The Empty Space: A Book About the Theatre: Deadly, Holy, Rough, Immediate*, New York: Atheneum.

Bruner, J. and R. W. Brown (1956), *A Study of Thinking*, New York: John Wiley & Sons.

Buelow, G. J. (2001), 'Affects, theory of the (Ger. *Affektenlehre*)', in *Grove Music Online*, DOI: https://doi.org/10.1093/gmo/9781561592630. article.00253.

Butler, S. (2015), *The Ancient Phonograph*, Princeton: Princeton University Press.

Butler, S. and S. Nooter, eds (2018), *Sound and the Ancient Senses*, London-New York: Routledge.

Butt, J. (2015), 'What is a "Musical Work"? Reflections on the Origins of the "Work Concept" in Western Art Music', in A. Rahmatian (ed.), *Concepts of Music and Copyright: How Music Perceives Itself and How Copyright Perceives Music*, 1–22, Cheltenham: Edward Elgar Publishing.

Butterworth, G. W., transl. (1919), *Clement of Alexandria: The Exhortation to the Greeks. The Rich Man's Salvation. To the Newly Baptized*, Cambridge, MA: Harvard University Press.

Cairns, D. (2019), 'Introduction: Emotion History and the Classics', in D. Cairns (ed.), *A Cultural History of the Emotions in Antiquity*, 1–16, London-New York-Oxford: Bloomsbury.

Carr, D. (2020), 'Teleology and the Experience of History', in A. Turner (ed.), *Reconciling Ancient and Modern Philosophies of History*, 311–26, Berlin: De Gruyter.

Casali, G. (2022), 'Rievocare la musica greca antica: Ettore Romagnoli e la collaborazione con Giuseppe Mulè per il Teatro greco di Siracusa', *Greek and Roman Musical Studies* 10 (1): 217–52.

Castaldo, D. (2009), 'Fonti classiche per le Nozze di Peleo e Teti', in F. Luisi (ed.), *Francesco Buti tra Roma e Parigi: Diplomazia, Poesia, Teatro*, 471–84, Roma: Torre d'Orfeo.

Castaldo, D. (2012), 'Amico Aspertini's Apollo and Muses in the Isolani Castle at Minerbio near Bologna', *Music in Art* 37: 71–82.

Castaldo, D. (2018), 'Images of Ancient Music in Jean-Jacques Boissard's Works', in T. Markovic and A. Baldassarre (eds), *Music Cultures in Sounds, Words and Images: Essays in Honor of Zdravko Blažeković*, 407–20, Wien: Hollitzer Wissenschaftverlag.

Castaldo, D. (2020), 'The Visual Heritage: Images of Ancient Music before and after the Rediscovery of Pompeii', in T. A. C. Lynch and E. Rocconi (eds), *A Companion to Ancient Greek and Roman Music*, 473–88, Hoboken, NJ: John Wiley & Sons.

Cattin, G. (1976), 'Nel quarto centenario di Nicola Vicentino teorico e compositore', *Studi musicali* 5: 29–57.

Cattin, G. (1981), 'Church Patronage of Music in Fifteenth Century Italy', in I. Fenlon (ed.), *Music in Medieval and Early Europe. Patronage, Sources and Texts*, 21–36, Cambridge: Cambridge University Press.

Chailley, J. (1960), *L'imbroglio des modes*, Paris: A. Leduc.

Chailley, J., ed. (1965), *Alia musica: traité de musique du IXe siècle*, Paris: Université de Paris.

Chaniotis, A. (2011), 'Festivals and Contests in the Greek World', in *Thesaurus Cultus et Rituum Antiquorum* 7: 1–43, 160–72, Los Angeles: The J. Paul Getty Museum.

Christensen, Th. (2018), 'Music Theory', in M. Everist and Th. Forrest Kelly (eds), *The Cambridge History of Medieval Music*, 357–81, Cambridge: Cambridge University Press.

Christenson, D. M. (2013), 'Eunuchus', in A. Augoustakis and A. Traill (eds), *A Companion to Terence*, 262–80, Chichester, WS: John Wiley & Sons.

Citroni, M. (2006), 'The Concept of the Classical and the Canons of Model Authors in Roman Literature', in J. I. Porter (ed.), *Classical Pasts: The Classical Traditions of Greece and Rome*, 204–34, Princeton: Princeton University Press.

Clarke, D. (2011), 'Musical Autonomy Revisited', in H. Clayton, T. Herbert and R. Middleton (eds), *The Cultural Study of Music: A Critical Introduction*, 2nd edn, 159–70, London: Routledge.

Cochrane, T., B. Fantini and K. R. Scherer, eds (2013), *The Emotional Power of Music: Multidisciplinary Perspectives on Musical Arousal, Expression, and Social Control*, Oxford: Oxford University Press.

Cohen, D. E. (2013), 'Rousseau as Music Theorist: Harmony, Mode, and (L'Unité de) Mélodie', *Journal of American Musicological Society* 66 (1): 175–80.

Cohen, D. E. (2022), 'Melodia and the "Disposition of the Soul": G. C. Monteverdi's "Platonic" Defense of the *Seconda Pratica*', *Journal of Musicology* 39 (2): 179–208.

Coleman, J. (1998), 'Some Relations between the Study of Aristotle's *Ethics*, *Rhetoric*, and *Politics* in Late Thirteenth- and Early Fourteenth-Century Arts Courses and the Justification of Contemporary Civic Activities (Italy and France)', in J. Canning and O. G. Oexle (eds), *Political Thought and the Realities of Power in the Middle Ages*, 127–57, Göttingen: Vandenhoeck and Ruprecht.

Colesanti, G. and L. Lulli, eds (2016), *Submerged Literature in Ancient Greek Culture 2: Case Studies*, Berlin-New York: De Gruyter.

Colesanti, G. and M. Giordano, eds (2014), *Submerged Literature in Ancient Greek Culture: An Introduction*, Berlin-New York: De Gruyter.

Conser, A. (2020), 'Pitch Accent and Melody in Aeschylean Song', *Greek and Roman Musical Studies* 8 (2): 254–78.

Cook, N. (2013), *Beyond the Score: Music as Performance*, New York: Oxford University Press.

Coplan, A. (2006), 'Catching Characters' Emotions: Emotional Contagion Responses to Narrative Fiction Film', *Film Studies* 8: 26–38.

Cox, V. (2021), 'Quintilian in the Italian Renaissance', in M. van Der Poel, M. Edwards and J. J. Murphy (eds), *The Oxford Handbook of Quintilian*, 359–79, Oxford: Oxford University Press.

Critchley, M. and R.A. Henson (1977), *Music and the Brain: Studies ion the Neurology and Music*, with a foreword by M. Tippet, London: W. Heinemann medical books.

Csapo, E. and P. Wilson (2009), 'Timotheus the New Musician', in F. Budelmann (ed.), *Cambridge Companion to Greek Lyric*, 277–93, Cambridge: Cambridge University Press.

Csapo, E. (2004), 'The Politics of the New Music', in P. Murray and P. Wilson (eds), *Music and the Muses: The Culture of* Mousike *in the Classical Athenian City*, 207–48, Oxford: Oxford University Press.

Curren, R. R. (2000), *Aristotle on the Necessity of Public Education*, Lanham: Rowman & Littlefield.

Curtis, L. and N. Weiss, eds (2021), *Music and Memory in the Ancient Greek and Roman Worlds*, Cambridge: Cambridge University Press.

van Damme, W. (1996), *Beauty in Context: Towards an Anthropological Approach to Aesthetics*, Leiden-New York- Köln: Brill.

D'Angour, A. (2006), 'Intimations of the Classical in Early Greek *Mousikē*', in J. I. Porter (ed.), *Classical Pasts: The Classical Traditions of Greece and Rome*, 89–105, Princeton: Princeton University Press.

D'Angour, A. (2011), *The Greeks and the New: Novelty in Ancient Greek Imagination and Experience*, Cambridge: Cambridge University Press.

D'Angour, A. (2020), '"Old" and "New" Music: The Ideology of *Mousikē*', in T. A. C. Lynch and E. Rocconi (eds), *A Companion to Ancient Greek and Roman Music*, 409–20, Hoboken, NJ: John Wiley & Sons.

D'Angour, A. (2021), 'Recreating the Music of Euripides' *Orestes*', *Greek and Roman Musical Studies* 9 (1): 175–90.

Da Col, P. (2018), 'Silent Voices: Professional Singers in Venice', in K. Schiltz (ed.), *A Companion to Music in Sixteenth-Century Venice*, 230–71, Leiden-Boston: Brill.

Da Rios, R., ed. and transl. (1957), *Aristoxeni Elementa Harmonica*, Roma: Ist. Poligrafico dello Stato.

Dalhaus, C. (1983 [1977]), *Foundations of Music History*, transl. by J. B. Robinson, Cambridge-London: Cambridge University Press (or. edn Köln: Hans Gerig).

Davies, S. (2010), 'Emotions Expressed and Aroused by Music: Philosophical Perspectives', in P. N. Juslin and J. A. Sloboda (eds), *The Oxford Handbook of Music and Emotion: Theory, Research, Applications*, 15–43, Oxford: Oxford University Press.

Davies, S. (2011), *Musical Understandings and Other Essays on the Philosophy of Music*, Oxford-New York: Oxford University Press.

Davies, S. (2013), 'Music-to-Listener Emotional Contagion', in T. Cochrane, B. Fantini and K. R. Scherer (eds), *The Emotional Power of Music: Multidisciplinary Perspectives on Musical Arousal, Expression, and Social Control*, 169–76, Oxford: Oxford University Press.

Delavaud-Roux, M.-H., eds (2019), *Corps et voix dans les danses du théâtre antique*, Rennes: Presses Universitaires de Rennes.

De Simone, M. (2008), 'The "Lesbian" Muse in Tragedy: Euripides *melopoiós* in Aristoph. *Ra.* 1301–28', *Classical Quarterly* 58 (2): 479–90.

De Simone, M. (2020), 'Music and Gender in Greek and Roman Culture: Female Performers and Composers', in T. A. C. Lynch and E. Rocconi (eds), *A Companion to Ancient Greek and Roman Music*, 397–408, Hoboken, NJ: John Wiley & Sons.

Decety, J. and A. N. Meltzoff (2011), 'Empathy, Imitation and the Social Brain', in A. Copland and P. Goldie (eds), *Empathy: Philosophical and Psychological Perspectives*, 58–81, New York: Oxford University Press.

Destiyanti, I. C. and S. Setiana (2020), 'Habituation Behavior to Enhance Student Learning', *Advances in Social Science, Education and Humanities Research* 410: 296–9.

Destrée, P. (2017), 'Aristotle and Musicologists on Three Functions of Music: A Note on *Pol.* 8, 1341b40–1', *Greek and Roman Musical Studies* 5 (1): 35–42.

Devine, A. M. and L. D. Stephens (1994), *The Prosody of Greek Speech*, Oxford: Oxford University Press.

DeWoskin, K. J. (1982), *A Song for One or Two: Music and the Concept of Art in Early China*, Ann Arbor, MI: The University of Michigan Press.

Dickreiter, M. (2000), 'The Structure of Harmony in Johannes Kepler's *Harmonice mundi* (1619)', in P. Gozza, (ed.), *Number to Sound: The Musical Way to the Scientific Revolution*, 173–88, Dordrecht-Boston-London: Kluwer Academic Publishers.

Diels, H. and W. Kranz, eds (1951), *Die Fragmente der Vorsokratiker*, 5th edn, Berlin: Weidmannsche (DK).

Dillon, J. M. and J. P. Hershbell, transl. (1991), *Iamblichus, On the Pythagorean Way of Life*, Atlanta, GA: Society of Biblical Literature.

Dorf, S. N. (2019), *Performing Antiquity: Ancient Greek Music and Dance from Paris to Delphi, 1890–1930*, Oxford-New York: Oxford University Press.

Dorf, S. N. (2021), 'The Ballets Russes and the Greek Dance in Paris: Nijinsky's *Faune*, Fantasies of the Past, and the Dance of the Future', in L. Gianvittorio-Ungar and K. Schlapbach (eds), *Choreonarratives:*

Dancing Stories in Greek and Roman Antiquity and Beyond, 284–99, Leiden-Boston: Brill.

Drago, A. (2017), 'What Was the Role of Galileo in the Century-Long Birth of Modern Science?', *Philosophia Scientiae* 21 (1): 35–54.

Durante, M. (1958), '*EPEA PTEROENTA*: La parola come "cammino" in immagini greche e vediche', *Rendiconti della Accademia Nazionale dei Lincei, Classe di Scienze Morali, Storiche e Filologiche* 13: 3–14.

Düring, I. (1934), *Ptolemaios und Porphyrios über die Musik*, Göteborg: Elanders.

Dutton, D. (2003), 'Authenticity in Art', in J. Levinson (ed.), *The Oxford Handbook of Aesthetics*, 258–74, Oxford: Oxford University Press.

Dyer, J. (2007), 'The Place of *Musica* in Medieval Classifications of Knowledge', *Journal of Musicology* 24 (1): 3–71.

Dyson, H. (2009), *Prolepsis and Ennoia in the Early Stoa*, Berlin-New York: De Gruyter.

Ekman, P. (1971), 'Constants across Cultures in the Face and Emotion', *Journal of Personality and Social Psychology* 17 (2): 124–39.

Emlyn-Jones, Ch. and W. Preddy, ed. and transl. (2013), *Plato. Republic, Volume I: Books 1-5*, Cambridge, MA: Harvard University Press.

Ercolani, A. and M. Giordano, eds (2016), *Submerged Literature in Ancient Greek Culture 3: The Comparative Perspective*, Berlin-Boston: De Gruyter.

Exarchos, D. (2018), 'The Skin of Spectral Time in Grisey's *Le Noir de l'Étoile*', *Twentieth-Century Music* 15 (1): 31–55.

Field, J. V. (1984), 'Kepler's Rejection of Numerology', in B. Vickers (ed.), *Occult Scientific Mentalities*, 273–96, Cambridge: Cambridge University Press.

Fix, A. (2019), '*Esperienza*, Teacher of All Things: Vincenzo Galilei's Music as Artisanal Epistemology', *Nuncius* 34: 535–74.

Ford, A. (2002), *The Origin of Criticism: Literary Culture and Poetic Theory in Classical Greece*, Princeton: Princeton University Press.

Ford, A. (2004), 'Catharsis: The Power of Music in Aristotle's *Politics*', in P. Wilson and P. Murray (eds), *Music and the Muses: The Culture of Mousike in the Classical Athenian City*, 309–36, Oxford: Oxford University Press.

Ford, A. (2015), 'The Purpose of Aristotle's *Poetics*', *Classical Philology* 110: 1–21.

Forgács, R. (2021), *Latin and Music in the Early Modern Era: Education, Theory, Composition, Performance and Reception*, Leiden-Boston: Brill.

Fortenbaugh, W. W. (2002 [1975]), *Aristotle on Emotion*, London: Duckworth (or. edn New York: Barnes & Noble).

Fortenbaugh, W. W. (2003), *Theophrastean Studies*, Stuttgart: Franz Steiner Verlag.

Fortenbaugh, W. W., P. M. Huby, R. W. Sharples and D. Gutas, eds (1992), *Theophrastus of Eresus: Sources for His Life, Writings, Thoughts and Influence*, 2 vols, Leiden-New York: Brill (FHS&G).

Franklin, J. C. (2002a), 'Harmony in Greek and Indo-Iranian Cosmology', *The Journal of Indo-European Studies* 30 (1/2): 1–25.

Franklin, J. C. (2002b), 'Aristophanes *Clouds*: A Reconstruction', in E. Hickmann, A. D. Kilmer and R. Eichmann (eds), *The Archaeology of Sounds: Origin and Organisation*, 661–4, Rahden, Westf.: Leidorf.

Franklin, J. C. (2015), *Kinyras: The Divine Lyre*, Washington DC: Center of Hellenic Studies.

Franklin, J. C. (2019), 'Behind the Schemes: UVM's Production of Euripides' *Helen* (March 22–25, 2018)', *Didaskalia* 15 (14), DOI: https://www. didaskalia.net/issues/15/14/.

Franklin, J. C. (2020), 'Ancient Greek Music and the Near East', in T. A. C. Lynch and E. Rocconi (eds), *A Companion to Ancient Greek and Roman Music*, 229–41, Hoboken, NJ: John Wiley & Sons.

Freese, J. H., transl., rev. by G. Striker (2020), *Aristotle: Art of Rhetoric*, Cambridge, MA: Harvard University Press.

Fumaroli, M. (2001), 'Les Abeilles et les Araignées', in A.-M. Lecoq (ed.), *La Querelle des Anciens et des Modernes: 17e-18e siècles*, Paris: Gallimard.

Gallo, F. A. (1995), *Music in the Castle: Troubadours, Books, and Orators in Italian Courts of the Thirteenth, Fourteenth, and Fifteenth Centuries*, Chicago-London: The University of Chicago Press.

Gallo, F. A. (1998), 'L'ottavo libro della *Politica* di Aristotele: il testo e le traduzioni. Indagine preliminare sulle fonti (XIII-XV secolo)', *Schede Medievali* 24–25: 118–26.

Gambassi, O. (1997), 'Pueri cantores' *nelle cattedrali d'Italia tra Medioevo e età moderna: Le scuole eugeniane. Scuole di canto annesse alle cappelle musicali*, Florence: Olschki.

Geary, J. (2006), 'Reinventing the Past: Mendelssohn's *Antigone* and the Creation of an Ancient Greek Musical Language', *Journal of Musicology* 23 (2): 187–226.

Geary, J. (2014), *The Politics of Appropriation: German Romantic Music and the Ancient Greek Legacy*, Oxford: Oxford University Press.

Gentili, B. (1988), *Poetry and Its Public in Ancient Greece: From Homer to the Fifth Century*, transl. with an intr. by A. Th. Cole, Baltimore-London: Johns Hopkins University Press.

Gentili, B. and F. Luisi (1995), 'La *Pitica* 12 di Pindaro e l'aulo di Mida', *Quaderni Urbinati di Cultura Classica* 49 (1): 7–31.

Gianvittorio-Ungar, L. and K. Schlapbach, eds (2021), *Choreonarratives. Dancing Stories in Greek and Roman Antiquity and Beyond*, Leiden-Boston: Brill.

Gianvittorio, L. (2018), 'New Music and Dancing Prostitutes. Performance and Imagery of Erotic Dancing in the Musical Criticism of Old Comedy', *Greek and Roman Musical Studies* 6 (2): 265–89.

Giles, R. H. (2016), 'The Inaudible Music of the Renaissance: From Marsilio Ficino to Robert Fludd', *Renaissance and Reformation/Renaissance et Réforme* 39 (2): 129–66.

von Glahn, D. and M. Broyles (2013), 'Art Music', in *Grove Music Online*, DOI: https://doi.org/10.1093/gmo/9781561592630.article.A2227279.

Goehr, L. (1992), *The Imaginary Museum of Musical Works*, Oxford: Oxford University Press.

Goldhill, S. and R. Osborne (1999), *Performance Culture and Athenian Democracy*, Cambridge: Cambridge University Press.

Gottlieb, P. (2021), *Aristotle on Thought and Feeling*, Cambridge: Cambridge University Press.

Gouk, P. (2002), 'The Role of Harmonics in the Scientific Revolution', in Th. Christensen (ed.), *The Cambridge History of Western Music Theory*, 223–45, Cambridge: Cambridge University Press.

Gozza, P. (2000), *Number to Sound: The Musical Way to the Scientific Revolution*, Dordrecht-Boston-London: Kluwer Academic Publishers.

Gracyk, Th. (2021), 'Hume's Aesthetics', in E. N. Zalta (ed.), *The Stanford Encyclopedia of Philosophy* (Winter 2021 Edition), DOI: https://plato.stanford.edu/archives/win2021/entries/hume-aesthetics/.

Granata, C. and N. Waanders (2015), "'Un'arpa grande tutta intagliata e dorata'. New Documents on the Barberini Harp', *Recercare* 27 (1/2): 139–64.

Griffith, M. (2020), 'Between Local and Global: Music and Cultural Identity in Ancient Greece', in T. A. C. Lynch and E. Rocconi (eds), *A Companion to Ancient Greek and Roman Music*, 381–96, Hoboken, NJ: John Wiley & Sons.

Grig, L. (2017), *Popular Culture in the Ancient World*, Cambridge: Cambridge University Press.

Grisey, G. (1990), *Le Noir de l'ètoile, pour six percussionistes, band magnétique et retransmission in situ de signaux astronomiques*, Milano: Universal Music Publishing Ricordi.

Gross, D. M. (2006), *The Secret History of Emotion: From Aristotle's Rhetoric to Modern Brain Science*, Chicago: University of Chicago Press.

Gross, D. M. (2010), 'Defending the Humanities with Charles Darwin's *The Expression of the Emotions in Man and Animals* (1872)', *Critical Inquiry* 37 (1): 34–59.

Gruen, E. S. (2011), *Rethinking the Other in Antiquity*, Princeton: Princeton University Press.

Guariento, L. (2018), 'From the Divine Monochord to the Weather-Glass: Changing Perspectives in Robert Fludd's Philosophy', in J. A. T. Lancaster and R. Raiswell (eds), *Evidence in the Age of the New Sciences*, 151–76, Berlin-Heidelberg: Springer.

Guidobaldi, N. (2007), *Presenze dell'Antico nell'immaginario musicale del Rinascimento*, Bologna: Il Mulino.

Guidobaldi, N. (2020), 'Rediscovery and "Invention" of Antiquity in the Humanistic Musical Imagination', in V. Minazzi and C. Ruini (eds), *Historical Atlas of Medieval Music*, 260–6, Turnhout: Brepols.

Gurd, S. A. (2019), *The Origins of Music Theory in the Age of Plato*, London-New York-Oxford: Bloomsbury.

Haar, J. (1961), *Musica mundana: Variations on a Pythagorean Theme*, Diss. Harvard University.

Haar, J. (2001), 'Music of the Spheres', in *Grove Music Online*, DOI: https://doi.org/10.1093/gmo/9781561592630.article.19447.

Hadjimichael, Th. A. (2019), *The Emergence of the Lyric Canon*, Oxford: Oxford University Press.

Hadot, I. (2005 [1984]), *Arts libéraux et philosophie dans la pensée antique. Contribution à l'histoire de l'éducation et de la culture dans l'antiquité*, Paris: Vrin (or. ed. Paris: Etudes augustiniennes).

Hagel, S. (2004), 'Calculating Auloi – the Louvre Aulos Scale', in E. Hickmann and R. Eichmann (eds), *Music-Archeological Sources: Excavated Finds, Oral Transmission, Written Evidence*, 373–90, Rahden, Westf.: Leidorf.

Hagel, S. (2010), *Ancient Greek Music: A New Technical History*, Cambridge: Cambridge University Press.

Hagel, S. (2012), 'How to Shoot an Aulos – Taking Measurements from Photographs', in R. Eichmann, J. Fang and L.-Ch. Kock (eds), *Sound from the Past: The Interpretation of Musical Artifacts in an Archaeological Context*, 405–13, Rahden, Westf.: Leidorf.

Hagel, S. (2020), 'Notation', in T. A. C. Lynch and E. Rocconi (eds), *A Companion to Ancient Greek and Roman Music*, 297–310, Hoboken, NJ: John Wiley & Sons.

Hagel, S. (2022), 'How Is Technology Useful in the Study of Ancient Music?', *Greek and Roman Musical Studies* 10 (2): 269–89.

Hagel, S. and Ch. Terzēs (2022), 'Two Auloi from Megara', *Greek and Roman Musical Studies* 10 (1): 15–77.

Haines, J. (2013), 'Antiquarian Nostalgia and the Institutionalization of Early Music', in C. Bithell and J. Hill (eds), *Oxford Handbook of Music Revival*, 73–93, Oxford: Oxford University Press.

Hall, E. (1989), *Inventing the Barbarian: Greek Self-Definition through Tragedy*, Oxford: Clarendon Press.

Hall, E. (2011), 'Putting the Class into Classical reception', in L. Hardwick and Ch. Stray (eds), *A Companion to Classical Receptions*, 386–98, Chichester, WS: John Wiley & Sons.

Hall, E. and F. Macintosh (2005), *Greek Tragedy and the British Theatre 1660–1914*, Oxford: Oxford University Press.

Hall, J. (2004), 'Cicero and Quintilian on the Oratorical Use of Hand Gestures', *Classical Quarterly* 54 (1): 143–60.

Hall, J. (2007), 'Oratorical Delivery and the Emotions: Theory and Practice', in W. Dominik and J. Hall (eds), *A Companion to Roman Rhetoric*, 218–34, Malden, MA-Oxford: John Wiley & Sons.

Halliwell, S. (2002), *The Aesthetics of Mimesis: Ancient Texts and Modern Problems*, Princeton: Princeton University Press.

Halliwell, S. (2011), *Between Ecstasy and Truth: Interpretations of Greek Poetics from Homer to Longinus*, Oxford-New York: Oxford University Press.

Halliwell, S. (2012), 'Amousia: Living without the Muses', in I. Sluiter and R. M. Rosen (eds), *Aesthetic Value in Classical Antiquity*, 15–45, Leiden-Boston: Brill.

Halliwell, S. (2017), 'Was Aristotle a Literary Historian?', in J. von Grethlein and A. Rengakos (eds), *Griechische Literaturgeschichtsschreibung. Traditionen, Probleme und Konzepte*, 189–211, Berlin-Boston: De Gruyter.

Halliwell, S., transl. (1995), *Aristotle, Longinus, Demetrius. Poetics. Longinus: On the Sublime. Demetrius: On Style*, transl. by S. Halliwell, W. Hamilton Fyfe, D. C. Innes, W. Rhys Roberts, Cambridge, MA: Harvard University Press.

Hamm, C., R. Walser, J. Warwick and Ch. H. Garrett (2014), 'Popular Music', in *Grove Music Online*, DOI: https://doi.org/10.1093/gmo/9781561592630.article.A2259148.

Hankins, J. (2015), 'Humanism and Music in Italy', in A. M. Busse Berger and J. Rodin (eds), *The Cambridge History of Fifteenth-Century Music*, 231–62, Cambridge: Cambridge University Press.

Hanslick, E. (1891 [1854]), *The Beautiful in Music: A Contribution to the Revisal of Musical Aesthetics*, London: Novello, Ewer and Company (or. edn Leipzig: Johann Ambrosius Barth).

Harriott, R. (1969), *Poetry and Criticism before Plato*, London: Methuen.

Harris, W. V. (2001), *Restraining Rage: The Ideology of Anger Control in Classical Antiquity*, Cambridge, MA: Harvard University Press.

Hatfield, E., J. T. Cacioppo and R. L. Rapson (1994), *Emotional Contagion*, Cambridge: Cambridge University Press; Paris: Editions de la Maison des Sciences de l'Homme.

Hatfield, E., R. L. Rapson and Y.-C. L. Le (2009), 'Emotional Contagion and Empathy', in J. Decety and W. Ickes (eds), *The Social Neuroscience of Empathy*, 19–30, Cambridge, MA-London: The MIT Press.

Hatfield, E., M. Carpenter and R. L. Rapson (2014), 'Emotional Contagion as a Precursor to Collective Emotions', in C. von Scheve and M. Salmela (eds), *Collective Emotions: Perspectives from Psychology, Philosophy, and Sociology*, 108–22, Oxford: Oxford University Press.

Haupt, P. (1919), 'The Harmony of the Spheres', *Journal of Biblical Literature* 38 (3/4): 180–3.

Henderson, J., ed. and transl. (1998a), *Aristophanes. Acharnians. Knights*, Cambridge, MA: Harvard University Press.

Henderson, J., ed. and transl. (1998b), *Aristophanes. Clouds. Wasps. Peace*, Cambridge, MA: Harvard University Press.

Henderson, J., ed. and transl. (2002), *Aristophanes. Frogs. Assembly Women. Wealth*, Cambridge, MA: Harvard University Press,

Hendrickson, G. L. and H. M. Hubbell (1939), *Cicero. Brutus. Orator*, Cambridge, MA: Harvard University Press.

Herington, J. (1985), *Poetry into Drama: Early Tragedy and the Greek Poetic Tradition*, Berkeley-Los Angeles-London, University of California Press.

Hett, W. S., transl. (1936), *Aristotle. Minor Works: On Colours. On Things Heard. Physiognomics. On Plants. On Marvellous Things Heard. Mechanical Problems. On Indivisible Lines. The Situations and Names of Winds. On Melissus, Xenophanes, Gorgias,* Cambridge, MA: Harvard University Press.

Hett, W. S., transl. (1957), *Aristotle. On the Soul. Parva Naturalia. On Breath*, Cambridge, MA: Harvard University Press.

Hicks, A. (2017), *Composing the World: Harmony in the Medieval Platonic Cosmos*, Oxford-New York: Oxford University Press.

Hoenig, Ch. (2020), 'Calcidius on Cosmic Harmony', in F. Pelosi and F. M. Petrucci (eds), *Music and Philosophy in the Roman Empire*, 262–85, Cambridge: Cambridge University Press.

Holst-Warhaft, G. (1980), *Theodorakis: Myth and Politics in Modern Greek Music*, Amsterdam: Hakkert.

Holst-Warhaft, G. (2001), 'Rebetika', in *Grove Music Online*, DOI: https://doi.org/10.1093/gmo/9781561592630.article.51102.

Holst-Warhaft, G. (2002), 'Politics and Popular Music in Modern Greece', *Journal of Political & Military Sociology* 30 (2): 297–323.

Huebner, S. (2021), 'Saint-Saëns and Sophocles', *Nineteenth-Century Music Review* 18: 499–519.

Huffmann, C. A. (1993), *Philolaus of Croton, Pythagorean and Presocratic*, Cambridge: Cambridge University Press.

Huffmann, C. A. (2005), *Archytas of Tarentum: Pythagorean, Philosopher and Mathematician King*, Cambridge: Cambridge University Press.

Huffmann, C. A. (2009), 'The Pythagorean Conception of the Soul', in D. Frede and R. Burkhard (eds), *Body and Soul in Ancient Philosophy*, 21–43, Berlin: De Gruyter.

Huffmann, C. A. (2010), 'Response to Barker', *Classical Philology* 105 (4): 420–5.

Huffmann, C. A. (2014), *A History of Pythagoreanism*, Cambridge: Cambridge University Press.

Hunkins, J. (2007–8), 'The Chronology of Leonardo Bruni's Later Works (1437–1443)', *Studi medievali e umanistici* 5/6: 1–40.

Huron, A. (2008), *Sweet Anticipation: Music and the Psychology of Expectation*, Cambridge, MA-London: The MIT Press.

Innes, D. C. and W. Rhys Roberts (1995), *Aristotle, Longinus, Demetrius. Poetics. Longinus: On the Sublime. Demetrius: On Style*, transl. by S. Halliwell, W. Hamilton Fyfe, D. C. Innes, W. Rhys Roberts, Cambridge, MA: Harvard University Press.

von Jan, K, ed. (1962 [1895]), *Musici scriptores Graeci: Aristoteles, Euclides, Nicomachus, Bacchius, Gaudentius, Alypius et melodiarum veterum quidquid exstat*, Hildesheim: Olms (or. edn Leipzig: Teubner).

Jones, E. M. (2012), 'Allocating Musical Pleasure: Performance, Pleasure, and Value in Aristotle's *Politics*', in I. Sluiter and R. M. Rosen (eds), *Aesthetic Value in Classical Antiquity*, 159–82, Leiden-Boston: Brill.

Juslin, P. N. (2019), *Musical Emotions Explained: Unlocking the Secrets of Musical Affect*, Oxford: Oxford University Press.

Juslin, P. N. and D. Västfjäll (2008), 'Emotional Responses to Music: The Need to Consider Underlying Mechanisms', *Behavioral and Brain Sciences* 31 (5): 559–75.

Käppel, L. K. (2006), 'Paean', in H. Cancik and H. Schneider (eds), *Brill's New Pauly*, DOI: http://dx.doi.org/10.1163/1574-9347_bnp_e903750.

Kassel, R. and C. Austin, eds (1983–), *Poetae Comici Graeci*, Berlin-Boston: De Gruyter (KA).

Katsanevaki, A. (2017), 'Modern Laments in Northwestern Greece: Their Importance in Social and Musical Life and the "Making" of Oral

Tradition', *Musicologist: An International Journal of Music Studies* 1 (1): 95–140.

Katsanevaki, A. (2023), 'The Evolutionary Pentatonism in Nicomachus, the Extant Fragments and an Ancient Greek Musical *Praxis*', *Greek and Roman Musical Studies* 11 (1): 139–81.

Kaufmann, H. W. and R. L. Kendrick (2001), 'Vicentino, Nicola', in *Grove Music Online*, DOI: https://doi.org/10.1093/gmo/9781561592630. article.29293.

Ketterer, R. C. (1999), 'Classical Sources and Thematic Structure in the Florentine *intermedi* of 1589', *Renaissance Studies* 13 (2): 192–222.

Ketterer, R. C. and J. Solomon (2017), 'Classics and Opera', in *Oxford Bibliographies online*, DOI: https://www.oxfordbibliographies.com/view/document/obo-9780195389661/obo-9780195389661-0264.xml.

Kivy, P. (2002), *Introduction to a Philosophy of Music*, Oxford: Clarendon Press.

Kjeller Johansen, Th. (2021), *Productive Knowledge in Ancient Philosophy: The Concept of* Technê, Cambridge-New York: Cambridge University Press.

Klavan, S. A. (2019), 'Hearing the λόγος: Diogenes of Babylon and the ἐπιστημονικὴ αἴσθησις', *Mnemosyne* 72 (6): 908–29.

Klavan, S. A. (2021), *Music in Ancient Greece: Melody, Rhythm and Life*, London-New York-Oxford: Bloomsbury.

Konstan, D. (2006), *The Emotions of the Ancient Greeks: Studies in Aristotle and Classical Literature*, Toronto-Buffalo-London: University of Toronto Press.

Kramarz, A. (2018), 'Christian Reception of the "New-Music" Debate in the Church Fathers and Clement of Alexandria', *Greek and Roman Musical Studies* 6 (2): 359–78.

Kristeller, P. O. (1981), *Renaissance Thought and the Arts: Collected Essays*, Princeton: Princeton University Press.

Lambropoulou, V. (1995–6), 'On Harmony: Etymology, Preplatonic Meanings and Elements', *Platon* 47–48: 179–93.

Landels, J. G. (1999), *Music in Ancient Greece and Rome*, London-New York, Routledge.

Lanzoni, S. (2018), *Empathy: A History*, New Haven, CT: Yale University Press.

Leith, S. (2011), *You Talkin' to Me? Rhetoric From Aristotle to Obama*, London: Profile Books.

Letoublon, F. (1999), 'Epea Pteroenta ("Winged Words")', *Oral Tradition* 14 (2): 321–35.

LeVen, P. A. (2010), 'New Music and Its Myths: Athenaeus' Reading of the *aulos* Revolution (*Deipnosophistae* 14.616e–617f)', *The Journal of Hellenic Studies* 130: 35–47.

LeVen, P. A. (2020), *Music and Metamorphosis in Graeco-Roman Thought*, Cambridge: Cambridge University Press.

Levidou, K., K. Romanou and G. Vlastos, eds (2016), *Musical Receptions of Greek Antiquity*, Cambridge: Cambridge Scholars Publishing.

Levitin, D. (2009), 'The Neural Correlates of Temporal Structure in Music', *Music and Medicine* 1: 9–13, DOI: 10.1177/1943862109338604.

Lévy, C. (2020), 'The *Scalae Naturae* and Music, Two Models in Philo's Thought', in F. Pelosi and F. M. Petrucci (eds), *Music and Philosophy in the Roman Empire*, 21–37, Cambridge: Cambridge University Press.

Lindley, M. (2001), 'Tuning', in *Grove Music Online*, DOI: https://doi.org/10.1093/gmo/9781561592630.article.28578.

Lloyd-Jones, H. (1982), *Blood for the Ghosts: Classical Influences in the Nineteenth and Twentieth Centuries*, London: Duckworth.

Lloyd, G. E. R. (1973), *Greek Science After Aristotle*, London: Chatto & Windus.

Lundberg, M. (2023), 'Meibom in Sweden, 1652–1653: Peeling the Historiographical Layers', in J. Kreslinsand and M. Lundberg (eds), *Marcus Meibom: Studies in the Life and Works of a Seventeenth-Century Polyhistor*, 27–52, Copenhagen: Museum Tusculanum Press.

Lynch, T. A. C. and E. Rocconi, eds (2020), *A Companion to Ancient Greek and Roman Music*, Hoboken, NJ: John Wiley & Sons.

Macaskill, G. (2013), *The Slavonic Text of 2 Enoch*, Leiden-Boston: Brill.

Mackridge, P. (2020), '"You used to sing all my songs": Poetry, Language and Song from Solomos to Seferis', in P. Tambakaki, P. Vlagopoulos, K. Levidou and R. Beaton (eds), *Music, Language, and Identity in Greece: Defining a National Art Music in the Nineteenth and Twentieth Centuries*, London-New York: Routledge.

McClure, L. (2003), *Courtesans at Table: Gender and Greek Literary Culture in Athenaeus*, London-New York: Routledge.

Mambella, G. (2015), *Gioseffo Zarlino e la scienza musicale del Cinquecento: dal numero sonoro al corpo sonoro*, Venezia: Ist. Veneto di Scienze.

Maor, E. (2018), *Music by the Numbers: From Pythagoras to Schoenberg*, Princeton: Princeton University Press.

Marenbon, J. (2021), 'Anicius Manlius Severinus Boethius', in E. N. Zalta (ed.), *The Stanford Encyclopedia of Philosophy* (Winter 2021 Edition), DOI: https://plato.stanford.edu/archives/win2021/entries/boethius/.

Maricchiolo, F., A. Gnisci and M. Bonaiuto (2012), 'Coding Hand Gestures: A Reliable Taxonomy and a Multi-media Support', in A. Esposito, A. M. Esposito, A. Vinciarelli, R. Hoffmann and V. C. Müller (eds), *Cognitive Behavioural Systems*, 405–16, Berlin-Heidelberg: Springer.

Marignetti, B. (1996), 'Gli intermedi della *Pellegrina*: repertori emblematici e iconologici', *Rivista Italiana di Musicologia* 31 (2): 281–301.

Martin, R. P. (2015), 'Festivals, Symposia, and the Performance of Greek Poetry', in P. Destrée and P. Murray (eds), *A Companion to Ancient Aesthetics*, 15–30, Chichester, WS: John Wiley & Sons.

Mason, A. (2016), *Ancient Aesthetics*, London: Routledge.

Mathiesen, Th. J. (1988), *Ancient Greek Music Theory: A Catalogue raisonné of Manuscripts*, Repertoire international des sources musicales B/XI, Munich: Henle.

Mathiesen, Th. J. (1999), *Apollo's Lyre: Greek Music and Music Theory in Antiquity and the Middle Ages*, Lincoln-London: University of Nebraska Press.

Mathiesen, Th. J. (2002), 'Greek Music Theory', in Th. Christensen (ed.), *The Cambridge History of Western Music Theory*, 109–35, Cambridge: Cambridge University Press.

Mayhew, R., ed. and transl. (2011), *Aristotle. Problems, Volume I: Books 1–19*, Cambridge, MA: Harvard University Press.

Meineck, P., W. M. Short and J. Devereaux, eds (2018), *The Routledge Handbook of Classics and Cognitive Theory*, London: Routledge.

Melidis, C. (2020), 'The Vocal Art in Greek and Roman Antiquity', in T. A. C. Lynch and E. Rocconi (eds), *A Companion to Ancient Greek and Roman Music*, 201–12, Hoboken, NJ: John Wiley & Sons.

Melini, R. (2008), 'Charles Burney e l'archeologia musicale dell'antica area vesuviana', *Philomusica* 7 (2): 83–107.

Menut, A. D. (1970), *Maistre Nicole Oresme, Le livre de Politiques d'Aristote, published from the Text of the Avranches Manuscript 223, with a Critical Introduction and Notes*, Philadelphia: The American Philosophical Society.

Meriani, A. (1995), 'Un "esperimento" di Pitagora (Nichom. *Harm. ench.* 6, pp. 245–248 Jan)', in B. Gentili and F. Perusino (eds), *Mousiké: Metrica, ritmica e musica greca in memoria di Giovanni Comotti*, 77–92, Pisa: Istituti editoriali e poligrafici internazionali.

Meriani, A. (2015), 'Notes on the *Prooemium in Musicam Plutarchi ad Titum Pyrrhynum* by Carlo Valgulio (Brescia 1507)', *Greek and Roman Musical Studies* 3: 116–36.

Meriani, A. (2016), 'Teoria e storia della musica greca antica alla scuola di Vittorino da Feltre', *Rivista di cultura classica e medioevale* 58 (2): 311–35.

Meriani, A. (2019), 'Carlo Valgulio studioso di musica greca antica: il *Prooemium in musicam Plutarchi ad Titum Pirrhynum* (Brescia 1507)', *Vichiana* 66 (1): 61–88.

Meriani, A. (2022), *Plutarchi Chaeronensis De musica Carolo Valgulio interprete*, Firenze: SISMEL Edizioni del Galluzzo.

Michon, P. (2016), 'Christian Rhythm at the End of Antiquity (4th–6th cent. AD), Part 6', *Rhuthmos* (1 September 2016), DOI: https://rhuthmos.eu/spip.php?article1983.

Michon, P. (2018), 'Rhythm as Aesthetic Criterion (Part 1)', *Rhuthmos* (5 November 2018), DOI: https://rhuthmos.eu/spip.php?article2281.

Miller, P. J. (2023), *Sport: Antiquity and Its Legacy*, London-New York-Oxford: Bloomsbury.

Miller, S. R. (2001), 'Stile antico (It.: "old style")', in *Grove Music Online*, DOI: https://doi.org/10.1093/gmo/9781561592630.article.26771.

Minar, E. L. (1961), *Plutarch. Moralia, Volume IX: Table-Talk, Books 7–9. Dialogue on Love*, Cambridge, MA: Harvard University Press,

Mohan, B. (2019), *Understanding Public Speaking: A Learner's Guide to Persuasive Oratory*, London: Routledge.

Montanari, F. (2017), 'The Idea of History of Literature: The Beginnings in Ancient Greek Culture', in J. von Grethlein and A. Rengakos (eds), *Griechische Literaturgeschichtsschreibung. Traditionen, Probleme und Konzepte*, 153–69, Berlin-Boston: De Gruyter.

Morelli, G. (2001), 'Il «classico» in musica, dal dramma al frammento', in
S. Settis (ed.), *I Greci. Storia, cultura, arte, società, 3: I Greci oltre la Grecia*,
1175–244, Torino: Einaudi.

Morfill, W. R. and R. H. Charles, ed. and transl. (1896), *The Book of the
Secrets of Enoch*, Oxford: Clarendon Press.

Mountford, (1936), 'The Music of Pindar's "Golden Lyre"', *Classical Philology*
31 (2): 120–36.

Mouyis, A. (2010), *Mikis Theodorakis: Finding Greece in His Music*, Corfu:
Kerkyra Publications.

Murray, A. T., transl., rev. by W. F. Wyatt (1925), *Homer. Iliad, Volume II:
Books 13–24*, Cambridge, MA: Harvard University Press.

Murray, P. (2014), 'The Muses in Antiquity', in K. W. Christian, C. E. L. Guest
and C. Wedepohl (eds), *The Muses and Their Afterlife in Post-Classical
Europe*, 13–32, London-Turin: The Warburg Institute and Nino Aragno
Editore.

Murray, P. (2015), 'Poetic Inspiration', in P. Destrée and P. Murray (eds),
A Companion to Ancient Aesthetics, 158–74, Chichester, WS: John
Wiley & Sons.

Murray, P. (2020), 'The Mythology of the Muses', in T. A. C. Lynch and
E. Rocconi (eds), *A Companion to Ancient Greek and Roman Music*,
13–24, Hoboken, NJ: John Wiley & Sons.

Nagy, G. (2020), 'On the Shaping of the Lyric Canon in Athens', in B. Currie
and I. Rutherford (eds), *The Reception of Greek Lyric Poetry in the
Ancient World: Transmission, Canonization and Paratext*, 95–111,
Leiden-Boston: Brill.

Napolitano, M. (2010), 'Greek Tragedy and Opera: Notes on a Marriage
Manqué', in P. Brown and S. Ograjenšek (eds), *Ancient Drama in Music
for the Modern Stage*, 31–46, New York: Oxford University Press.

Neri, C. (2021), 'Letteratura popolare', in *Folkloricum: Archive of Ancient
Folklore*, DOI: https://www.folkloricum.it/letteratura-popolare/.

Nettl, B. (2001), 'Music', in *Grove Music Online*, DOI: https://doi.
org/10.1093/gmo/9781561592630.article.40476.

Nietzsche, F. W. (2013 [1870]), *The Greek Music Drama*, transl. by P. Bishop,
intro by J. Marsden, New York: Contra Mundum Press.

Nolan, C. (2002), 'Music Theory and Mathematics', in Th. Christensen (ed.), *The Cambridge History of Western Music Theory*, 272–304, Cambridge: Cambridge University Press.

Norlin, G., transl. (1929), *Isocrates. On the Peace. Areopagiticus. Against the Sophists. Antidosis. Panathenaicus*, Cambridge, MA: Harvard University Press.

North Fowler, H., transl. (1926), *Plato. Euthyphro. Apology. Crito. Phaedo. Phaedrus*, Cambridge, MA: Harvard University Press,

Norton, C. E., transl. (1892), *The Divine Comedy, Volume 3, Paradise by Dante Alighieri*, Boston: Houghton Mifflin Company.

Novokhatko, A. (2020), 'The Origins and Growth of Scholarship in Pre-Hellenistic Greece', in F. Montanari (ed.), *History of Ancient Greek Scholarship: From the Beginnings to the End of the Byzantine Age*, 9–131, Leiden-Boston: Brill.

Obbink, D. (1995), *Philodemus and Poetry: Poetic Theory and Practice in Lucretius, Philodemus, and Horace*. Oxford: Oxford University Press.

Olson, S. D., ed. and transl. (2011), *Athenaeus. The Learned Banqueters, Volume VII: Books 13.594b–14*, Cambridge, MA: Harvard University Press.

Olson, S. D., transl. and comm. (2014), *Fragmenta Comica. Eupolis frr. 326–497, Fragmenta incertarum fabularum, Fragmenta dubia*, Heidelberg: Verlag Antike.

Page, D. L. (1962), *Poetae Melici Graeci*, Oxford: Clarendon Press.

Palisca, C. V. (1977), *Girolamo Mei 1519–1594, Letters on Ancient and Modern Music to Vicenzo Galilei and Giovanni Bardi: A Study With Annotated Texts*, Cambridge-Rome: American Institute of Musicology.

Palisca, C. V. (1985), *Humanism in Italian Renaissance Musical Thought*, New Haven-London: Yale University Press.

Palisca, C. V. (1989), *The Florentine Camerata: Documentary Studies and Translations*, New Haven-London: Yale University Press.

Palisca, C. V. (1993), 'Aristoxenus Redeemed in the Renaissance', *Revista de Musicología* 16 (3): 1283–93.

Palisca, C. V. (2001a), 'Zarlino, Gioseffo', in *Grove Music Online*, DOI: https://doi.org/10.1093/gmo/9781561592630.article.30858.

Palisca, C. V. (2001b), 'Prima pratica', in *Grove Music Online*, DOI: https://doi.org/10.1093/gmo/9781561592630.article.22350.

Palisca, C. and P. Barbieri (2001), 'Doni, Giovanni Battista', in *Grove Music Online*, DOI: https://doi.org/10.1093/gmo/9781561592630.article.08001.

Panegyres, K. (2017), 'The Ethnic Elements of Greek Music', *TAPA* 147: 235–319.

Panti, C. (2020), 'The Reception of Greek Music Theory in the Middle Ages: Boethius and the Portraits of Ancient Musicians', in T. A. C. Lynch and E. Rocconi (eds), *A Companion to Ancient Greek and Roman Music*, 449–60, Hoboken, NJ: John Wiley & Sons.

Parry, R. (2014), '*Episteme* and *Techne*', in E. N. Zalta (ed.), *The Stanford Encyclopedia of Philosophy*, Fall 2014 Edition, DOI: http://plato.stanford.edu/archives/fall2014/entries/episteme-techne/.

Pasler, J. (2001), 'Postmodernism', in *Grove Music Online*, DOI: https://doi.org/10.1093/gmo/9781561592630.article.40721.

Pasticci, S., ed. (2019), 'Ildebrando Pizzetti: Sulle tracce del modernismo italiano', *CHIGIANA: Journal of Musicological Studies* 49.

Pegg, C. (2001), 'Folk Music', in *Grove Music Online*, DOI: https://doi.org/10.1093/gmo/9781561592630.article.09933.

Pelosi, F. (2010), *Plato on Music, Soul and Body*, Cambridge: Cambridge University Press.

Pelosi, F. (2016), 'Music for Life: Embryology, Cookery and *Harmonia* in the Hippocratic *On Regimen*', *Greek and Roman Musical Studies* 4 (2): 191–208.

Pelosi, F. (2017), 'Against Musical ἀτεχνία: Papyrus Hibeh I 13 and the Debate on τέχνη in Classical Greece', *Apeiron* 50 (3): 393–413.

Pelosi, F. (2018), 'Eight Singing Sirens Heavenly Harmonies in Plato and the Neoplatonists', in J. Prins and M. Vanhaelen (eds), *Sing Aloud Harmonious Spheres: Renaissance Conceptions of Cosmic Harmony*, 15–30, New York-London: Routledge.

Pelosi, F. (2020a), 'Musical Imagery in Clement of Alexandria and Origen: The Greek Musical World Revised and Accepted', in F. Pelosi and F. M. Petrucci (eds), *Music and Philosophy in the Roman Empire*, 155–77, Cambridge: Cambridge University Press.

Pelosi, F. (2020b), 'Music and Emotions', in T. A. C. Lynch and E. Rocconi (eds), *A Companion to Ancient Greek and Roman Music*, 337–50, Hoboken, NJ: John Wiley & Sons.

Pelosi, F. and F. M. Petrucci (2020), *Music and Philosophy in the Roman Empire*, Cambridge: Cambridge University Press.

Peponi, A.-E. (2012), *Frontiers of Pleasure: Models of Aesthetic Response in Archaic and Classical Greek Thought*, Oxford: Oxford University Press.

Petrucci, F. M. (2020), 'The Harmoniser God: Harmony as a Cosmological Model in Middle Platonist Theology', in F. Pelosi and F. M. Petrucci (eds), *Music and Philosophy in the Roman Empire*, 60–84, Cambridge: Cambridge University Press.

Piazza, L. (2019), 'Il paradigma dell'arte sinestetica: la rinascita della messa in scena tragica al Teatro greco di Siracusa', *Sinestesieonline* 25: 12–19.

Pietschmann, K. and J. Steichen (2015), 'Musical Institutions in the Fifteenth Century and Their Political Contexts', in A. M. Busse Berger and J. Rodin (eds), *The Cambridge History of Fifteenth-Century Music*, 403–26, Cambridge: Cambridge University Press.

Pirrotta, N. (1968), 'Dante musicus: Gothicism, Scholasticism, and Music', *Speculum: A Journal of Mediaeval Studies* 43: 245–57.

Pirrotta, N. and E. Povoledo (1982), *Music and Theatre from Poliziano to Monteverdi*, transl. by K. Eales, Cambridge: Cambridge University Press.

Pöhlmann, E. (1970), *Denkmäler Altgriechischer Musik: Sammlung, Übertragung und Erläuterung Aller Fragmente und Fälschungen*, Nürnberg: H. Carl.

Pöhlmann, E. and M. L. West (2001), *Documents of Ancient Greek Music*, Oxford: Oxford University Press (*DAGM*).

Politis, N. (2010 [1871]), 'Study on the Life of Modern Greeks', in A. Ersoy, M. Górny and V. Kechriotis (eds), *Modernism: Representations of National Culture*, 3–8, Budapest: CEU Press (or. edn Athens: τύποις Σαραντάκος Οἰκονόμου).

Porter, J. I. (2010), *The Origins of Aesthetic Thought in Ancient Greece*, Cambridge: Cambridge University Press.

Porter, J. I. (2018), 'Sounds You Cannot Hear: Cicero and the Tradition of Sublime Criticism', in T. Phillips and A. D'Angour (eds), *Music Text & Culture in Ancient Greece*, 203–32, Oxford: Oxford University Press.

Power, T. (2020), 'New Music in New York: Notes on a Recent *Herakles*, Rescored', *Greek and Roman Musical Studies* 8 (1): 200–6.

Power, T. (2022), 'Are You Experienced? Recent Approaches to the Study of Music in Greek and Roman Religion', *Greek and Roman Musical Studies* 10 (2): 327–56.

Powers, H. S. and F. Wiering (2001), 'Mode (II)', in *Grove Music Online*, DOI: https://doi.org/10.1093/gmo/9781561592630.article.43718.

Prauscello, L. (2014), *Performing Citizenship in Plato's* Laws, Cambridge: Cambridge University Press.

Prins, J. (2012), 'The Music of the Pulse in Marsilio Ficino's *Timaeus* Commentary', in M. Horstmanshoff, H. King and C. Zittel (eds), *Blood, Sweat and Tears: The Changing Concepts of Physiology from Antiquity into Early Modern Europe*, 393–413, Leiden-Boston: Brill.

Prins, J. (2015), *Echoes of an Invisible World: Marsilio Ficino and Francesco Patrizi on Cosmic Order and Music Theory*, Leiden-Boston: Brill.

Prins, J. and M. Vanhaelen, eds (2018), *Sing Aloud Harmonious Spheres Renaissance Conceptions of Cosmic Harmony*, New York-London: Routledge.

Provenza, A. (2012), 'Aristoxenus and Music Therapy: Fr. 26 Wehrli within the Tradition on Music and Catharsis', in C. A. Huffmann (ed.), *Aristoxenus of Tarentum. Discussion*, 91–128, Piscataway, NJ: Transaction Publishers.

Provenza, A. (2014), 'Soothing Lyres and *epodai*: Music Therapy and the Cases of Orpheus, Empedocles and David', in J. Goodnick Westenholz, Y. Maurey and E. Seroussi (eds), *Music in Antiquity: The Near East and the Mediterranean*, 298–339, Berlin: De Gruyter.

Provenza, A. (2020), 'Music and Medicine', in T. A. C. Lynch and E. Rocconi (eds), *A Companion to Ancient Greek and Roman Music*, 351–64, Hoboken, NJ: John Wiley & Sons.

Psaroudakēs, S. (2013), 'The Daphnē Aulos', *Greek and Roman Musical Studies* 1: 93–121.

Psaroudakēs, S. (2020), 'Lyre and Aulos from an Athenian Classical Grave in the Area between the So-Called "Eriai" Gates and the Dipylon (Grave 48, 470–50 BC)', *Greek and Roman Musical Studies* 8 (1): 11–44.

Psaroudakēs S., D. Marini, A. Georgaki, G. Kouroupetroglou, S. Polychronopoulos and K. Bakogiannis (2021), 'Physical Modeling of the Ancient Greek Wind Musical Instrument Aulos: A Double-Reed Exciter Linked to an Acoustic Resonator', *IEEExplore* 9: 98150–60.

Rackham H., transl. (1926), *Aristotle. Nicomachean Ethics*, Cambridge, MA: Harvard University Press.

Rackham H., transl. (1942), *Cicero. On the Orator: Book 3. On Fate. Stoic Paradoxes. Divisions of Oratory*, Cambridge, MA: Harvard University Press.

Raffa, M. (2017), 'Voce e strumenti in alcune "Questioni di armonia" del corpus aristotelico', *Il saggiatore musicale* 24: 7–22.

Raffa, M. (2020), 'Music in Greek and Roman Education', in T. A. C. Lynch and E. Rocconi (eds), *A Companion to Ancient Greek and Roman Music*, 311–22, Hoboken, NJ: John Wiley & Sons.

Rash, R. (2002), 'Tuning and Temperament', in Th. Christensen (ed.), *The Cambridge History of Western Music Theory*, 193–222, Cambridge: Cambridge University Press.

Readhead, L. and V. Hawes, eds (2016), *Music and/as Process*, Cambridge: Cambridge Scholars Publishing.

Reinach, Th. (1894), 'Conférence sur la musique grecque et l'hymne à Apollon', *Revue des études grecques* 7: 24–42.

Renger, A.-B. and A. Stavru, eds (2016), *Pythagorean Knowledge from the Ancient to the Modern World: Askesis, Religion, Science*, Wiesbaden: Harrasowitz Verlag

Restani, D. (1983), 'Il *Chirone* di Ferecrate e la "nuova" musica greca: Ricerca sul lessico retorico-musicale', *Rivista italiana di musicologia* 18 (2): 139–92.

Restani, D. (1990), *L'itinerario di Girolamo Mei: dalla Poetica alla musica con un'appendice di testi*, Florence: Olschki.

Restani, D. (2001), 'Girolamo Mei et l'héritage de la dramaturgie antique dans la culture musicale de la seconde moitié du XVIe siècle', in F. Decroisette, F. Frontisi and J. Heuillon (eds), *La naissance de l'Opera: Euridice 1600–2000*, 57–96, Paris: L'Harmattan.

Restani, D. (2011a), 'Il *De musica* attribuito a Plutarco e Girolamo Mei', *Quaderni Urbinati di Cultura Classica* 99 (3): 259–70.

Restani (2011b), 'Musica per educare: modelli antichi e recezioni moderne', in L. Mauro and A. Campodonico (eds), *L'uomo (in)formato: Percorsi nella paideia ieri e oggi*, 43–58, Milano: Franco Angeli.

Restani, D. (2012), 'L'eredità musicale del Mondo antico', in P. Fabbri e M. C. Bertieri (eds), *Musica e società 1: Dall'Alto Medioevo al 1640*, 229–97, Napoli: McGraw Hill.

Restani, D. (2015), 'Theory and Musical Performance of the Chorus in Sixteenth-Century Italy. A Case Study: Vicenza 1585', *Skenè: Journal of Theatre and Drama Studies* 1: 75–100.

Restani. D. (2019a), 'Embryologie, numérologie et musica humana: Un nouveau regard sur les sources et la réception du concept', in S. Conte, A. Oïffer-Bomsel and E. Cantarino-Suñer (eds), *Boèce au fil du temps: Son influence sur les lettres européennes du Moyen Âge à nos jours*, 135–56, Paris: Classiques Garnier.

Restani, D. (2019b), 'Listening between Lines: Alexander's Musical Legacy in Italy (13th–15th centuries)', in R. Strohm (ed.), *The Music Road: Coherence and Diversity in Music from the Mediterranean to India*, 87–100, London: Oxford University Press for the British Academy.

Restani, D. (2020), 'Ancient Greek Music in Early Modern Italy: Performance and Self-Representation', in T. A. C. Lynch and E. Rocconi (eds), *A Companion to Ancient Greek and Roman Music*, 461–72, Hoboken, NJ: John Wiley & Sons.

Rocconi, E. (2003), *Le parole delle Muse*, Rome: Quasar.

Rocconi, E. (2006), 'Women Players in Ancient Greece. The Context of Symposium and the Socio-Cultural Position of *Psaltriai* and *Auletrides* in the Classical World', in E. Hickmann, A. A. Both and R. Eichmann (eds), *Music Archaeology in Contexts: Archaeological Semantics, Historical Implications, Socio-Cultural Connotations*, 335–44, Rahden, Westf.: Leidorf.

Rocconi, E. (2011), '*Psychikē* e *ourania harmonia*: per un'ipotesi sulle fonti di Ps.-Plut. *De mus.* 1138c–1140b', *Quaderni Urbinati di Cultura Classica* 99 (3): 99–115.

Rocconi, E. (2012), 'The Aesthetic Value of Music in Platonic Thought', in I. Sluiter and R. M. Rosen (eds), *Aesthetic Value in Classical Antiquity*, 113–32, Leiden-Boston: Brill.

Rocconi, E. (2014), 'Effetti speciali sonori e mimetismo musicale nelle fonti greche', *Annali della Scuola Normale Superiore di Pisa, Classe di Lettere e Filosofia* 5: 703–19.

Rocconi, E. (2016a), 'The Music of the *Laws* and the Laws of Music: *Nomoi* in Music and Legislation', *Greek and Roman Musical Studies* 4 (1): 71–89.

Rocconi, E. (2016b), 'Traces of Folk Music in Ancient Greek Drama', in G. Colesanti and L. Lulli (eds), *Submerged Literature in Ancient Greek Culture, Vol. 2: Case Studies*, 339–51, Berlin-New York: De Gruyter.

Rocconi, E. (2019a), 'Music and Dance', in D. Cairns (ed.), *A Cultural History of the Emotions in Antiquity*, 47–61, London-New York-Oxford: Bloomsbury.

Rocconi, E. (2019b), '"Greek" versus "Barbarian" Music: The Self-Definition of Hellenic Identity through the Culture of *Mousikē*', in R. Eichmann, M. Howell and G. Lawson (eds), *Music and Politics in the Ancient World: Exploring Identity, Agency, Stability and Change through the Records of Music Archaeology*, 281–96, Berlin: Edition Topoi.

Rocconi, E. (2020), 'Music and the Soul', in D. C. Wolfsdorf (ed.), *Early Greek Ethics*, 612–28, Oxford: Oxford University Press.

Rocconi, E. (2021), 'La musica popolare', in *Folkloricum: Archive of Ancient Folklore*, DOI: https://www.folkloricum.it/musica-popolare/.

Rocconi, E. (2022a), 'Musical *Eisagōgai*', in A. Motta and F. M. Petrucci (eds), *Isagogical Crossroads from the Early Imperial Age to the End of Antiquity*, 183–204, Leiden-Boston: Brill.

Rocconi, E. (2022b), 'The Orator and the Dancer: Conceptualizing Gestures in Roman Performances', in K. Schlapbach (ed.), *Aspects of Roman Dance Culture*, 269–84, Stuttgart, Franz Steiner Verlag.

Rocconi, E. (2023), '83. Cardinal Bessarion's Manuscript of Ancient Greek Music Theory', in V. Borghetti and T. Shephard (eds), *The Museum of Renaissance Music: A History in 100 Exhibits*, Turnhout: Brepols.

Rocconi, E. and T. A. C. Lynch (2020), 'Introduction', in T. A. C. Lynch and E. Rocconi (eds), *A Companion to Ancient Greek and Roman Music*, 1–9, Hoboken, NJ: John Wiley & Sons.

Rodríguez López, M. I. and C. Romero Mayorga (2019), 'The Reception of Hellenistic Musical Iconography in the Iberian Art: The Patera of Santisteban del Puerto', *Music in Art* 44: 5–18.

Romani Mistretta, M. (2017), 'Hermes the Craftsman: The Invention of the Lyre', *GAIA. Revue interdisciplinaire sur la Grèce ancienne* 20: 5–22.

Roochnik, D. (2022), 'Ancient *Mousikē*: *Technē* or *Epistēmē*? Music as *Technē* in Book 8 of Aristotle's *Politics*', *Greek and Roman Musical Studies* 10 (2): 290–305.

Rose, V., ed. (1863), *Aristotelis qui ferebantur librorum fragmenta*, Leipzig: Teubner.

Rosenwein, B. H. (2002), 'Worrying about Emotions in History', *American Historical Review* 107: 821–45.

Rosenwein, B. H. (2006), *Emotional Communities in the Early Middle Age*, Ithaca, NY: Cornell University Press.

Rosenwein, B. H. (2010), 'Problems and Methods in the History of Emotions', *Journal for the History and Theory of Emotions* 1: 1–32.

Rossi, L. E. (1971), 'I generi letterari e le loro leggi scritte e non scritte nelle letterature classiche', *Bulletin of the Institute of Classical Studies* 18: 69–94.

Rossi, L. E. (2000), 'La letteratura alessandrina e il rinnovamento dei generi letterari della tradizione', in R. Pretagostini (ed.), *La letteratura ellenistica: Problemi e prospettive di ricerca*, 149–61, Rome: Quasar.

Rowland, I. D., transl. (1999), *Vitruvius: Ten Books on Architecture*, comm. and ill. by Th. N. Howe, with add. comm. by I. D. Rowland and M. J. Dewar, Cambridge: Cambridge University Press.

Rush, R. (2002), 'Tuning and Temperament', in Th. Christensen (ed.), *The Cambridge History of Western Music Theory*, 193–222, Cambridge: Cambridge University Press.

Sacks, O. (2007), *Musicophilia: Tales of Music and the Brain*, New York-Toronto: Alfred A. Knopf.

Sarti, S. (2020), 'Musical Heroes', in T. A. C. Lynch and E. Rocconi (eds), *A Companion to Ancient Greek and Roman Music*, 61–74, Hoboken, NJ: John Wiley & Sons.

Sassi, M. M. (2015), 'How Musical was Heraclitus' Harmony? A Reassessment of 22 B 8, 10, 51 DK', *Rhizomata* 3 (1): 3–25.

Scheffler, I. (1989 [1973]), *Reason and Teaching*, Indianapolis, IN: Hackett.

Schein, S. L. (2011), '"Our Debt to Greece and Rome": Canon, Class and Ideology', in L. Hardwick and Ch. Stray (eds), *A Companion to Classical Receptions*, 75–85, Chichester, WS: John Wiley & Sons.

Scherer, K. R. (2009), 'Emotion Theories and Concepts (Psychological Perspectives)', in D. Sander and K. R. Scherer (eds), *Oxford Companion to Emotion and the Affective Sciences*, 145–9, Oxford: Oxford University Press.

Scherer, K. R. and E. Coutinho (2013), 'How Music Creates Emotion: A Multifactorial Process Approach', in T. Cochrane, B. Fantini and

K. R. Scherer (eds), *The Emotional Power of Music: Multidisciplinary Perspectives on Musical Arousal, Expression, and Social Control*, 121–45, Oxford: Oxford University Press.

Schippers, H. (2010), *Facing the Music: Shaping Music Education from a Global Perspective*, Oxford: Oxford University Press.

Schülz, V. (2020), 'The Music of the Words in Roman Rhetoric', in T. A. C. Lynch and E. Rocconi (eds), *A Companion to Ancient Greek and Roman Music*, 365–78, Hoboken, NJ: John Wiley & Sons.

Schütrumpf, E. (2014a), 'The Earliest Latin Translations of Aristotle – William of Moerbeke', in E. Schütrumpf, *The Earliest Translations of Aristotle's* Politics *and the Creation of Political Terminology*, 9–25, Leiden-Boston: Brill.

Schütrumpf, E. (2014b), 'Bruni's Translation of Aristotle's *Politics*', in E. Schütrumpf, *The Earliest Translations of Aristotle's* Politics *and the Creation of Political Terminology*, 33–8, Leiden-Boston: Brill.

Schütrumpf, E., P. Stork, J. von Ophuijsen and S. Prince, ed. and transl. (2008), *Heraclides of Pontus: Text and Translation*, London: Routledge.

Semenzato, C. (2017), *À l'écoute des Muses en Grèce archaïque: la question de l'inspiration dans la poésie grecque à l'aube de notre civilization*, Berlin-Boston: De Gruyter.

Shapiro, L. and Sh. Spaulding (2021), 'Embodied Cognition', in E. N. Zalta (ed.), *The Stanford Encyclopedia of Philosophy* (Winter 2021 Edition), DOI: https://plato.stanford.edu/archives/win2021/entries/embodied-cognition/.

Shiloah, A. (1979–2003), *The Theory of Music in Arabic Writings (c. 900–1900)*, 2 vols. Répertoire International des Sources Musicales BX–BXa, Munich: G. Henle Verlag.

Shiloah, A. (2018), 'Theory of Cosmic Harmony in Jewish and Muslim Sources', in J. Prins and M. Vanhaelen (eds), *Sing Aloud Harmonious Spheres Renaissance Conceptions of Cosmic Harmony*, 44–61, New York-London: Routledge.

Siegel, H., D. C. Phillips and E. Callan (2018), 'Philosophy of Education', in E. N. Zalta (ed.), *The Stanford Encyclopedia of Philosophy* (Winter 2018 Edition), DOI: https://plato.stanford.edu/archives/win2018/entries/education-philosophy/.

Singer, P. N. (2022), 'What is a Pathos? Where Medicine Meets Philosophy', in G. Kazantzidis and D. Spatharas (eds), *Medical Understandings of Emotions in Antiquity*, 17–42, Berlin: De Gruyter.

Skeris, R. A. (1976), *ΧΡΩΜΑ ΘΕΟΥ: On the Origins and Theological Interpretation of the Musical Imagery Used by the Ecclesiastical Writers of the First Three Centuries, with Special Reference to the Image of Orpheus*, Altötting: Alfred Coppenrath.

Small, Ch. (1998), *Musicking: The Meanings of Performing and Listening*, Hanover, NH: Wesleyan University Press.

Solomon, J. (2010), 'The Reception of Ancient Greek Music in the Late Nineteenth Century', *International Journal of the Classical Tradition* 107 (4): 497–525.

Solomon, J. (2013), 'Opera and Greek Tragedy', in H. M. Roisman (ed.), *Encyclopedia of Greek Tragedy*, 918–24, Malden, MA: John Wiley & Sons.

Solomon, J. (2016), 'Read All About It! Ancient Greek Music Hits American Newspapers, 1875–1938', in R. Montemorra Marvin and C. Bashford (eds), *The Idea of Art Music in a Commercial World*, 202–22, Woodbridge: Boydell Press.

Spitzer, L. (1944), 'Classical and Christian Ideas of World Harmony Prolegomena to an Interpretation of the Word "Stimmung" (Part I)', *Traditio* 2: 409–64.

Spitzer, L. (1945), 'Classical and Christian Ideas of World Harmony Prolegomena to an Interpretation of the Word "Stimmung" (Part II)', *Traditio* 3: 307–64.

van Staden, H. (1989), *Herophilus: The Art of the Medicine in Early Alexandria*, Cambridge: Cambridge University Press.

Starr, G. G. (2013), *Feeling Beauty: The Neuroscience of Aesthetic Experience*, Cambridge, MA-London: The MIT Press.

Stearns, P. N. and C. Z. Stearns (1984), 'Emotionology: Clarifying the History of Emotions and Emotional Standards', *The American Historical Review* 90 (4): 813–36.

Steiner, D. (2013), 'The Gorgons' Lament: Auletics, Poetics, and Chorality in Pindar's *Pythian 12*', *American Journal of Philology* 134 (2): 173–208.

Steinmann, C. (2021), *Nachklänge, Instrumente der griechischen Klassik und ihre Musik. Materialien und Zeugnisse von Homer bis heute*, Basel-Berlin: Schwabe Verlag.

Storey. I. C., ed. and transl. (2011), *Fragments of Old Comedy, Volume I: Alcaeus to Diocles*, Cambridge, MA: Harvard University Press.

Stueber, K. (2019), 'Empathy', in E. N. Zalta (ed.), *The Stanford Encyclopedia of Philosophy* (Fall 2019 Edition), DOI: https://plato.stanford.edu/archives/fall2019/entries/empathy/.

Sun, X. and J. Che (2019), 'Cross-Cultural Empirical Aesthetics', in M. Nadal and O. Vartanian (eds), *The Oxford Handbook of Empirical Aesthetics*, Oxford: Oxford University Press, DOI: https://doi.org/10.1093/oxfordhb/9780198824350.013.41.

Tambakaki, P. (2019), '"Art-Popular" Song and Modern Greek Poets – Interactions and Ideologies: The Case of Mikis Theodorakis', in D. Tragaki (ed.), *Made in Greece: Studies in Popular Music*, 55–64, London: Routdledge.

Tambakaki, P., P. Vlagopoulos, K. Levidou, R. Beaton, eds (2020), *Music, Language and Identity in Greece: Defining a National Art Music in the Nineteenth and Twentieth Centuries*, London-New York: Routdledge.

Taplin, O. and R. Wyles (2010), *The Pronomos Vase and Its Context*, Oxford-New York: Oxford University Press.

Tarán, L. (1981), *Speusippus of Athens: A Critical Study with a Collection of the Related Texts and Commentary*, Leiden: Brill.

Terzēs, Ch. (2013), 'The Daphnē Harp', *Greek and Roman Musical Studies* 1: 123–49.

Terzēs, Ch. (2020), 'Musical Instruments of Greek and Roman Antiquity', in T. A. C. Lynch and E. Rocconi (eds), *A Companion to Ancient Greek and Roman Music*, 213–28, Hoboken, NJ: John Wiley & Sons.

Teske, R. J., transl. (1990), *The Works of Saint Augustine: Epistulae. Letters 100–155*, New York: Boniface Ramsey.

Teske, R. J., transl. (2004), *The Works of Saint Augustine: Epistulae. Letters 156–210*, New York: Boniface Ramsey.

Thaut, M. H. and D. A. Hodges, eds (2021), *The Oxford Handbook of Music and the Brain*, Oxford: Oxford University Press.

Theodorakis, M. (1982), *Machomeni Koultoura*, Athens: Synchroni Epochi.

Theodorakis, M. (2007), 'Συμπαντική αρμονία [Universal harmony]', in Γ. Κουγιουμουτζάκης (ed.), Συμπαντική αρμονία, μουσική και επιστήμη στον Μίκη Θεοδωράκη, Ηράκλειο: Πανεπιστημιακές Εκδόσεις Κρήτης.

Tocco, A. (2019), 'New Music and Early Peripatetic Scholarship: The "Degeneration" of Music as a Historiographical Turning Point', *Greek and Roman Musical Studies* 7 (1): 33–50.

Toner, J., ed. (2016), *A Cultural History of the Senses in Antiquity*, London-Oxford-New York-New Dehli-Sydney: Bloomsbury.

Tovanen, J., ed. (2022), *Forms of Representation in the Aristotelian Tradition. Volume One: Sense Perception*, Leiden-Boston: Brill.

Trabattoni, F. (2023), *From Death to Life: Key Themes in Plato's* Phaedo, Leiden-Boston: Brill.

Tredennick, H., transl. (1933), *Aristotle. Metaphysics, Volume I: Books 1–9*, Cambridge, MA: Harvard University Press.

Tredennick, H., transl. (1935), *Aristotle. Metaphysics, Volume II: Books 10–14. Oeconomica. Magna Moralia*, transl. by H. Tredennick and G. C. Armstrong, Cambridge, MA: Harvard University Press.

Troiani, S. (2022a), 'Ettore Romagnoli traduttore delle *Baccanti*: Tra lessico operistico e ricreazione ritmico-musicale del dramma antico', *Greek and Roman Musical Studies* 10 (1): 189–216.

Troiani, S. (2022b), *Dal testo alla scena e ritorno: Ettore Romagnoli e il teatro greco*, Trento: Università degli Studi di Trento – Dipartimento di Lettere e Filosofia.

Trost, W. and P. Vuilleumier (2013), 'Rhythmic Entrainment as a Mechanism for Emotion Induction by Music', in T. Cochrane, B. Fantini and K. R. Scherer (eds), *The Emotional Power of Music: Multidisciplinary Perspectives on Musical Arousal, Expression, and Social Control*, 213–25, Oxford: Oxford University Press.

Valentini, V. (1992), *La tragedia moderna e mediterranea: Sul teatro di Gabriele D'Annunzio*, Milano: Franco Angeli.

Vanhaelen, M. (2018), 'Cosmic Harmony, Demons, and the Mnemonic Power of Music in Renaissance Florence: The Case of Marsilio Ficino', in J. Prins and M. Vanhaelen (eds), *Sing Aloud Harmonious Spheres: Renaissance Conceptions of Cosmic Harmony*, 101–22, London-New York: Routledge.

Varela, F., E. Thompson and E. Rosch (1991), *The Embodied Mind: Cognitive Science and Human Experience*, Cambridge, MA-London: The MIT Press.

Vendries, Ch., ed. (2019), *Cornua de Pompeii: Trompettes romaines de la gladiature*, Rennes: Presses Universitaires de Rennes.

Vendrix, Ph. (2008), *Music and Mathematics in Late Medieval and Early Modern Europe*, Turnhout: Brepols.

Vergados A. (2014), 'Etymologie und Aitiologie bei Hesiod: die Musennamen in der Theogonie', in C. Reitz and A. Walter (eds), *Dichtung und Ursache: Strukturen aitiologischen Denkens*, 105–40, Hildesheim-Zürich-New York: Olms.

Vergados, A. (2013), *The Homeric Hymn to Hermes: Introduction, Text and Commentary*, Berlin: De Gruyter.

Viltanioti, I.-F. (2015), *L'harmonie des Sirènes du pythagorisme ancien à Platon*, Leiden-Boston: Brill.

Vlassopoulos, K. (2013), *Greeks and Barbarians*, Cambridge: Cambridge University Press.

Walker, D. P. (1958), *Spiritual and Demonic Magic from Ficino to Campanella*, London: Warburg Institute-University of London.

Walker, D. P. (1967), 'Kepler's Celestial Music', *Journal of the Warburg and Courtauld Institutes* 30: 228–50.

Walker, D. P., ed. (1963), *Les fêtes du mariage de Ferdinand de Médicis et de Christine de Lorraine, Florence, 1589: Musique des intermèdes de 'La pellegrina'*, Paris: Ed. du Centre national de la recherche scientifique.

Wehrli, F., ed. (1945), *Die Schule des Aristoteles: Texte und Kommentar. 2. Aristoxenos*, Basel-Stuttgart: B. Schwabe.

Weiss, N. A. (2020), 'Ancient Greek *Choreia*', in T. A. C. Lynch and E. Rocconi (eds), *A Companion to Ancient Greek and Roman Music*, 161–72, Hoboken, NJ: John Wiley & Sons.

Wessels, A. B. and J. J. H. Klooster, eds (2022), *Inventing Origins? Aetiological Thinking in Greek and Roman Antiquity*, Leiden-Boston: Brill.

West, M. L. (1992), *Ancient Greek Music*, Oxford: Clarendon Press.

Wilberding, J., ed. (2021), *World Soul: A History*, Oxford: Oxford University Press.

Wilson, P. (2007), 'Pronomos and Potamon: Two Pipers and Two Epigrams', *The Journal of Hellenic Studies* 127: 141–9.

van Wymeersch, B. (2014), 'The Muses and Musical Inspiration in Early Modern France: The Case of Pontus de Tyard and Mersenne Jan Söffne', in K. W. Christian, C. E. L. Guest and C. Wedepohl (eds), *The Muses and Their Afterlife in Post-Classical Europe*, 155–68, London: Warburg Institute.

Winnington-Ingram, R. P. (1963), *Aristidis Quintiliani De musica libri tres*, Leipzig: Teubner.

Wiskus, J. (2015), 'Temporalité et rythme musical dans *Les Confessions* de Saint Augustin', in L. Angelino (ed.), *Quand le geste fait sens*, 179–91, Sesto S. Giovanni: Édition Mimésis.

Wolfram, G. (2021), 'The Byzantine Modal System in Relation to Ancient Greek Music Theory', *IMS-RASMB, Series Musicologica Balcanica* 1 (2), DOI: https://doi.org/10.26262/smb.v1i2.7940.

Woodruff, P. (2015), 'Mimesis', in P. Destrée and P. Murray (eds), *A Companion to Ancient Aesthetics*, 329–40, Chichester, WS: John Wiley & Sons.

Yatromanolakis, D. (2009), 'Ancient Greek Popular Song', in F. Budelmann (ed.), *The Cambridge Companion to Greek Lyric*, 263–76, Cambridge: Cambridge University Press.

Yatromanolakis, D. and P. Roilos (2003), *Towards a Ritual Poetics*, Athens: Foundation of the Hellenic World.

Young C. (2020), 'Re-Awakening Mercury's Cithara: A Closer Look at Federico's Cetra', *Music in Art* 45: 25–51.

Zaidel, D. W. (2019), 'The Evolution of Aesthetics and Beauty', in M. Nadal and O. Vartanian (eds), *The Oxford Handbook of Empirical Aesthetics*, Oxford: Oxford University Press, DOI: https://doi.org/10.1093/oxfordhb/9780198824350.013.8.

Zeki, S. (1997), 'The Woodhull Lecture: Visual Art and the Visual Brain', *Proceedings of the Royal Institution of Great Britain* 68: 29–63.

Zeki, S. (1999), *Inner Vision: An Exploration of Art and the Brain*, Oxford: Oxford University Press.

Zeki, S. (2001), 'Artistic Creativity and the Brain', *Science* 293: 51–2.

General Index